The Four Articles of Prague within the Public Sphere of Hussite Bohemia

Czech Theological Perspectives

Series Editor: Dr. Jan Blahoslav Lášek (Charles University, Prague); Dr. Jacob Marques Rollison (Independent Scholar)

This series aims to constitute a distinguished forum for research issuing from or concerning Czech theology in the broadest sense of this compound term. Examples of research sought and welcomed under this umbrella include: high quality original monographs and edited volumes presenting research conducted by Czech scholars, in Czech universities, or in Czech territory; research conducted by non-Czech scholars or outside of Czech universities and territory which examines contemporary or historical theological trends and events linked to the Czech lands, people, and church (such as the Bohemian Reformation, the legacy of Jan Hus, etc.); and scholarly translations of both contemporary research and works of enduring theological or historical value which aim to fill out the currently sparse anglophone resources on these same topics. While Anglophone discussion is well acquainted with the historical and theological contours of the Reformation in Western Europe (especially France, Switzerland, and Germany), it has yet to fully attend to the importance of Czech theological history and Czech voices in contemporary theology. Wider recognition that this history and these voices are important in their own right (and not merely as precursors to Luther or Calvin) drives the posture of inquiry, listening, and dialogue which this series aims to embody.

Titles in the Series

The Four Articles of Prague within the Public Sphere of Hussite Bohemia

On the 600th Anniversary of Their Declaration (1420–2020)

Kamila Veverková

Translated by Angelo Shaun Franklin

LEXINGTON BOOKS

Lanham • Boulder • New York • London

Published by Lexington Books
An imprint of The Rowman & Littlefield Publishing Group, Inc.
4501 Forbes Boulevard, Suite 200, Lanham, Maryland 20706
www.rowman.com

6 Tinworth Street, London SE11 5AL, United Kingdom

British Library Cataloguing in Publication Information Available

Library of Congress Cataloging-in-Publication Data

Names: Veverková, Kamila, author. | Franklin, Angelo Shaun, translator. | Jacobellus, de Misa, -1429. Čtyři články pražské. English.
Title: The Four articles of Prague within the public sphere of Hussite Bohemia : on the 600th anniversary of their declaration (1420-2020) / Kamila Veverková ; translated by Angelo Shaun Franklin.
Other titles: Čtyři pražské články ve veřejném prostoru husitských Čech. English
Description: Lanham : Lexington Books, 2021. | Translation of: Čtyři pražské články ve veřejném prostoru husitských Čech. | Includes bibliographical references and index.
Identifiers: LCCN 2020044799 (print) | LCCN 2020044800 (ebook) | ISBN 9781793637727 (cloth ; permanent paper) | ISBN 9781793637734 (epub)
Subjects: LCSH: Hussites. | Jacobellus, de Misa, -1429. Čtyři články pražské. | Reformation—Early movements. | Bohemia (Czech Republic)—Church history. | Czech Republic—History—To 1500.
Classification: LCC BX4915.2 .V4813 2021 (print) | LCC BX4915.2 (ebook) | DDC 284/.3—dc23
LC record available at https://lccn.loc.gov/2020044799
LC ebook record available at https://lccn.loc.gov/2020044800

♾️™ The paper used in this publication meets the minimum requirements of American National Standard for Information Sciences—Permanence of Paper for Printed Library Materials, ANSI/NISO Z39.48-1992.

Contents

Preface

The question has often been posed as to whether or not the Hussite movement and its ideological development actually belong within the conceptual framework of the European Reformation.[1] Kamila Veverková's insightful work answers that pertinent question with a resounding *yes*: the Hussite movement truly belongs within the overall trajectory of the social and theological framework of Reformation history.[2] The so-called European Reformation certainly transformed societal structures, forged political alliances, and created new social relationships. Yet the Hussite Reformation had already effected such significant changes 100 years before the Reformation of the sixteenth century.

In most studies on the Reformation (often based on German research in particular), there has been a common tendency to view the Hussite movement as a pre-Reformation movement. In the second half of the twentieth century, the renowned professor and Reformation historian Amedeo Molnár (1923–1990) suggested an alternative periodization of the Reformation. According to Molnár, it proceeded in two waves: the first Reformation began with the Waldensian movement and culminated in the Hussite movement, while the second groundswell of the Reformation was the quintessential sixteenth-century European Reformation. The most important theological principle for the first Reformation was following the law of Christ (*lex Christi*); for the second reformation, the threefold *solas* necessary for salvation were emphasized: *sola gratia*, *sola Scriptura*, and *sola fide*.

Like the later European Reformation, the Czech Reformation was not entirely uniform. Nevertheless, it had an umbrella program which was found in the *Four Articles of Prague*, making this latter one of the central texts of the Czech Reformation. Veverková's work on the *Four Articles* is not merely a historical account; it depicts the historical circumstances leading to the formulation of the *Four Articles of Prague* and lists their theological sources, of course, but her work is also interdisciplinary and focuses on the Articles' political and legal impact and their principal importance in transforming medieval society. The Hussite program from 1420 contained values which later played a large role in the early modern age and in the Enlightenment. This program contributed to the transformation of the medieval world and to the emancipation of society from a legal dependence upon the Church.

In line with the theological emphasis on the *lex Dei*, the law of God was perceived as being intricately woven into every aspect and detail of life.[3] From this perspective, since the law of God reigns supreme, the word of God should be proclaimed freely (as stipulated in the first article); the church should not govern secular affairs (third article); and the sins of all people should be punished in a righteous way without making unfair distinctions based on social status (fourth article). In order for justice to be rendered according to the word of God, the laity should be allowed to participate in receiving communion under both kinds (*sub utraque specie*) since it is vitally necessary for salvation (second article). Despite various factions, all Hussite parties surprisingly agreed on this agenda. This program was present in various forms in Hussite Bohemia until the violent dissolution of the Reformation in 1620, when the Counter-Reformation represented by the ruling Habsburg monarchy prevailed in Bohemia.

Appropriately appearing on the occasion of the 600th anniversary of the *Four Articles'* public declaration in July 1420, Veverková's book seeks to answer two important questions: *how* and *to what extent* did the Hussite movement influence the transformation of Bohemia and the legal development of its constitution? From the Hussite perspective, when the law of God was followed in sincere obedience and actually put into practice, society was necessarily transformed. This transformation prepared the way for social advancements which led to the spread of modern values such as freedom and the equality of all people. In this light, the Hussite movement represents an important step within the history of modern political thought, premodern human rights, and the concept of an open society. Veverková concisely and compellingly explains the major emphasis of the confessional developments in the Kingdom of Bohemia in the fifteenth century and draws appropriate attention to the Treaty of Kutná Hora (1483), which enabled the free confession of two denominations which existed in the country (i.e., Catholics and Hussites-Utraquists). From the perspective of religious freedom, even with the principle of *cuius regio, eius religio* ("whose country, whose religion") expressed in the Peace of Augsburg (1555), the later European Reformation did not attain such heights. Religious freedom was subsequently brought about quite differently in various nation-states by the Enlightenment.

Furthermore, although *the Four Articles of Prague are more than six centuries old, they are perhaps surprisingly relevant to controversial modern concerns: the freedom of speech (first article), the freedom of conscience and religion (second article), the separation of church and state (third article), and equality under the law (fourth article).*[4] Veverková highlights the importance of the Four Articles of Prague in shaping modern political theories, showing how they contributed to the emancipation of society from the Church without infringing upon confessional freedom of religion.

Veverková's work is one of the first monographs to appear in English concerning the *Four Articles of Prague* and serves as a helpful introductory text for those who have a special interest in Bohemian history. Since the general facts of the Hussite movement are well-known from a variety of excellent works by Frederick Heymann, Matthew Spinka, David Schaff, Howard Kaminsky, and also in recent works by Thomas A. Fudge, this work is not a comprehensive treatise on the Hussite movement; it aims to provide a window into understanding certain aspects of the Hussite movement.[5] These general facts are interpreted in Veverková's work in a way which draws the reader's attention to their profound social impact not only in their own era, but also and above all their significance for the present day—a time when Christianity is attempting to navigate in murky waters and find a new orientation within contemporary society. This book not only concerns the intellectual heritage of Jan Hus and his followers, but generally encourages ethical reflection about how Christians are supposed to live directly in the heart and center of society and the example which they can draw from the Hussite era. As such, this volume is intended to invite the reader into deeper dialogue. Veverková's presentation complements existing anglophone approaches to the Bohemian Reformation. Our goal in presenting this translation in today's *lingua franca* is to provide new insights from a parallel yet unheard conversation to readers who are limited to only English language resources. Furthermore, this monograph carefully presents the ecclesiastical history of the Czech state in a widely understandable manner for a broader audience interested in Bohemian history, yet without any detraction from an academic or professional form in terms of research.

As the title indicates, the main strength of Veverková's book lies in its emphasis on the influence of the *Four Articles* upon the legal, political, religious, and cultural environment of their era. The *Four Articles* served as a foundation of future legal developments in Bohemia and also provided a viable example for the rest of Europe during the period of its transition from feudalism up until the rise of modern nation-states. In her conclusion, Veverková astutely notes that the legal aspects of the Bohemian Reformation can provide "a model for investigating and discovering legal rights within the complex postmodern age where states and nations are searching for a tolerable and beneficial form of contemporary coexistence." Our sincere hope is that this English translation of her valuable work will not only help to promote a deeper understanding of the *Four Articles of Prague*, but will also inspire further studies concerning the Hussite movement in particular, the significant personalities of that epoch, and the intriguing relationships between ancient, medieval, modern, and postmodern concepts of law, justice, authority, equality, human rights, society, and freedom.

Angelo Shaun Franklin and Jan Blahoslav Lášek
Prague, July 2020

NOTES

1. See Amedeo Molnár, *Die Waldenser—Geschichte und europäisches Ausmass einer Ketzerbewegung* (Göttingen: Vandenhoeck & Ruprecht, 1980); Amedeo Molnár, "Husovo místo v evropské reformaci," in *Československý časopis historický* 14/1 (1966): 1–14; Amedeo Molnár, "Der Hussitismus als christliche Reformbewegung," in Ferdinand Seibt, ed., *Bohemia sacra. Das Christentum in Böhmen, 973–1973* (Düsseldorf: Verlag Schwann, 1974), 92–109; Robert Kalivoda, *Husitská ideologie* (Prague: ČSAV, 1961); Martin Nodl, "The Hussites and the Bohemian Reformation," in *From Hus to Luther: Visual Culture in the Bohemian Reformation (1380–1620)*, eds., Kateřina Horníčková and Michal Šroněk (Turnhout: Brepols, 2016), 17–46; see also František Šmahel, *Husitské Čechy: Struktury, Procesy, Ideje* (Prague: Nakladatelství Lidové noviny, 2001).

2. For debates concerning the periodization of the "late medieval church" in relation to the "Reformation," see Natalia Nowakowska, "Reform before Reform? Religious Currents in Central Europe, c. 1500," in *A Companion to the Reformation in Central Europe*, eds. Howard Louthan and Graeme Murdock (Leiden: Brill, 2015), 121–143.

3. For various understandings of the law of God in relation to Hussitism, see: Martin Dekarli, "The Law of Christ (*Lex Christi*) and the Law of God (*Lex Dei*)—Jan Hus's Concept of Reform," in *The Bohemian Reformation and Religious Practice*, vol. 10, eds. Zdeněk V. David and David R. Holeton (Prague: Filosofia, 2015), 49–69; Thomas A. Fudge, "Hussite Theology and the Law of God," in *The Cambridge Companion to Reformation Theology*, eds., David Bagchi and David C. Steinmetz (Cambridge: Cambridge University Press, 2004), 22–27; Thomas A. Fudge, "The 'Law of God': Reform and Religious Practice in Late Medieval Bohemia," in *The Bohemian Reformation and Religious Practice* 1 (1994): 49–72; Howard Kaminsky, *A History of the Hussite Revolution* (Berkeley: University of California Press, 1967), 64–72, 118–125, 140–151, 296–309; Bernhard Töpfer, "Lex Christi, dominium und kirchliche Hierarchie bei Johannes Hus im Vergleich mit John Wyklif," in *Jan Hus— Zwischen Zeiten, Völkern, Konfessionen: Vorträge des internationalen Symposions in Bayreuth vom 22. bis 26. September 1993*, Ferdinand Seibt et al., eds (München: R. Oldenbourg, 1997), 157–165.

4. For a helpful evaluation of the modern issues, see Thomas K. Johnson, ed., *Global Declarations on Freedom of Religion or Belief and Human Rights* (Eugene: Wipf and Stock, 2017).

5. For other available English resources providing either very brief summaries of the Four Articles of Prague or the related overall historical context, see: Hugh LeCaine Agnew, *The Czechs and the Lands of the Bohemian Crown* (Stanford: Hoover Institution Press, 2004), 39–54; Zdeněk V. David, *Finding the Middle Way: The Utraquists' Liberal Challenge to Rome and Luther* (Baltimore: Johns Hopkins University Press, 2003), 25–26, 38–40, 61, 79, 234; Thomas A. Fudge, *Origins of the Hussite Uprising: The Chronicle of Laurence of Březová (1414–1421)* (London: Routledge, 2020), 113–116; Jeanne E. Grant, *For the Common Good: The Bohemian Land Law and the Beginning of the Hussite Revolution* (Leiden: Brill, 2015), 76–107; Frederick Heymann, *John Žižka and the Hussite Revolution* (Princeton: Princeton University Press, 1955), 148–163; Kaminsky, *A History of the Hussite Revolution*, 369–375; František Šmahel, "The Hussite Revolution (1419–1471)," in *A History of the Czech Lands*, eds. Jaroslav Pánek, Oldřich Tůma et al., 2nd ed. (Prague: Karolinum Press, 2018), 157–183; František Šmahel, *Creeds and Confessions of Faith in the Christian Tradition*, 3 vols., eds. Jaroslav Pelikan and Valerie R. Hotchkiss (New Haven: Yale University Press, 2003), 1:791–795.

Translator's Note

I have translated the text of the *Four Articles* presented here from the Czech text found in the critical edition of Rudolf Říčan entitled *Čtyři vyznání: vyznání Augsburské, Bratrské, Helvetské a České: Se 4 vyznáními staré církve a se Čtyřmi články pražskými.*[1] Since all major differences and textual variants are discussed in that volume, the reader looking for more detail on the various manuscripts is encouraged to consult the explanation in Říčan's introduction. Most of the introduction in *Čtyři vyznání* has been translated and included below, since it should provide a brief but sufficient background for the intended audience of this book. I have provided alternative translations of certain Czech words in editorial footnotes and have included the sources for all citations mentioned within the text of the *Four Articles*. Thanks are due to the Digital Library of Written Cultural Heritage for facilitating my access to these manuscripts.[2]

When the word *estates* in this text is lower-case letters it is used to delineate the distinct individual *estates*—the nobility, the knights, and the burghers; when it appears with a capital *"E"* (*Estates*), it denotes the collective association of the three groups. Almost all of the foreign names remain here in their original form, except for a few exceptions such as Sigismund and Charles which have been Anglicized due to their familiarity in anglophone discussions.

NOTES

1. Rudolf Říčan et al., eds., *Čtyři vyznání: vyznání Augsburské, Bratrské, Helvetské a České: Se 4 vyznáními staré církve a se Čtyřmi články pražskými* (Praha: Komenského evangelická fakulta bohoslovecká, 1951), 35–52.
2. See their website: https://www.manuscriptorium.com.

Part I

THE *FOUR ARTICLES OF PRAGUE*

Introduction to the *Four Articles of Prague*[1] (1951)

The first confession of the Bohemian Reformation was essentially the special program of the incipient Hussite movement expressed in the well-known *Four Articles of Prague*. The origin of these *Articles* and specifically formulated statements can be properly ascribed to Mikuláš of Pelhřimov in the autumn of 1419, when they were agreed upon by participants of rural pilgrimage camps and Praguers. However, all four demands contained in the *Articles* are an expression of the Bohemian religious movement since the time of Jan Milíč of Kroměříž. This is based on the assumption that the requirement for the Lord's Supper to be administered under both kinds to all believers (which had already been presented in 1414) was the result of the earlier desire to fully participate in the sacramental grace of communion as frequently as possible, and at the same time as a consequence of the principle that the law of Christ is the arbiter over every human tradition. The *Four Articles* expressed the convictions which had already been shared by a broad spectrum of the Hussite people; theologians expressed the articles in Latin and supported them not only from the Scriptures but also from various teachers of the ancient and medieval church. The significance of the specific program presented by the Hussite movement in the *Four Articles* was that it was founded upon certain requirements which were to be promoted, upheld, and realized in the church. In the program of the *Four Articles,* Christianity is presented as a commitment which provides direction and orientation for the whole of life. However, the demand for preaching the word of God primarily means declaring the grace of God, and it is the Lord's Supper in particular which continually reconfirms this message. And the moral requirements placed upon the lives of the priests and other estates implied that the grace which was received could only be espoused through a devout and obedient faith.

The Hussite program, however, was not uniform and straightforward, and from its very beginning evidenced varying degrees of decisiveness and purposefulness. Even the order of the *Four Articles* expressed the level of importance which the different Hussite factions attached to their content, and the textual emendations, even though negligible from the perspective of particular wording, reveal a gradual mitigation of the original program, which was officially narrowed and incorporated into a certain arrangement. The already amended *Four Articles* became the official manifesto of the Prague community and the Hussite Czechs in general in their negotiations with Sigismund both before the Battle of Vítkov Hill (Žižkov) on July 14, 1420, and also afterward; additionally, after another emendation, they became the provincial law at the Diet of Čáslav on June 7, 1421.

We are publishing the text of the *Articles* in the form in which it was publicized in 1844 in Czech by František Palacký in *Archiv český III*.[2] It is based on "a couple of old manuscripts" (yet without Palacký stating which ones) and appears to be the text from the beginning of July 1420. We have compared that text with the version in the university manuscript O.39 (fols. 124[a]–127[a]) of the Library of the Metropolitan Chapter of Prague, which probably was one of the sources that Palacký used among others.[3] We have inexplicitly corrected some of the apparent printing mistakes of Palacký. We have compared the Latin text of *Historia Hussitica* by Lawrence of Březová[4] with the manuscripts III.G.16 and IV.H.17 (fols. 65[a]–67[a]) from the National Library of the Czech Republic and noted the minor deviations. Elsewhere we state the differences in content of this version from 1420 compared with the older text of the *Articles* as presented in its basic formulation by Mikuláš of Pelhřimov in his *Kronika táborská*.[5] The German version[6] contained in the message of the Praguers to the German armies besieging Prague in July 1420 and the Latin text in manuscript D.53 (fols. 361[a]–371[a]) from the Metropolitan Chapter has already been noted as being much more extensive by Jaroslav Goll in a note on Lawrence's text and was reprinted by Bartoš, yet without documentation on the second article.[7] Finally, we consider the records from the Diet of Čáslav as represented by Palacký in *Archiv český III*, where again only the basic version of the *Four Articles* is recorded.[8] Therefore, we can assert that the following edition presented here is the most complete Czech edition of the *Four Articles of Prague* that has been published thus far. Professor F. M. Bartoš deserves our gratitude for assisting us in finding a few relevant passages from various ecclesiastical authors.

Every major work concerning the history of the Hussite movement has discussed the *Four Articles of Prague*: for example, František Palacký in the third volume of his *Dějiny národu českého v Čechách a v Moravě* (*History of the Czech Nation in Bohemia and Moravia*),[9] Václav Vladivoj Tomek in the fourth volume of his twelve-volume work *Dějepis města Prahy* (*The History of Prague*),[10] Friedrich von Bezold in his book on the history of Hussitism,[11] and Ferdinand Hrejsa in the second volume of his six-volume history of Christianity in the Czech lands.[12] František Dvorský attempted to place their origin as early as 1417 in his work on the articles.[13] Václav Novotný concluded that the origin of the *Four Articles* derived from the Czech religious movement in his review of *Die Genesis der vier Prager Artikel (The Origin of the Four Articles of Prague)* by Mathilde Uhlirz.[14] František Michálek Bartoš offered a portrait of the period in which the articles originated in his *Do čtyř pražských artikulů (Towards the Four Articles: The Intellectual and Constitutional Struggles between 1415–1420)*[15] and later retraced them in the manifestos of Praguers in *Manifesty města Prahy z doby husitské (Manifestos of Prague from the Hussite Era)*,[16] where he examined the opinions and conclusions of Josef Pekař on the articles in his work *Žižka a jeho doba (Jan Žižka and His Epoch)*.[17]

NOTES

1. This is a slightly abridged translation of the introduction in Rudolf Říčan et al., eds., *Čtyři vyznání*, 37–38.

2. František Palacký, *Archiv český, čili, Staré písemné památky české i morawske: z archivůw domácích i cizích* (W Praze: Stawy Králowstwj Českého, 1844), 3:213–216.

3. This is according to the opinion of F. M. Bartoš in *Manifesty města Prahy z doby husitské*; *Sborník příspěvků k dějinám hlavního města Prahy* (Praha: Obec hlavního města Prahy, 1932), 261–262. fn. 25–26.

4. *Fontes rerum bohemicarum*, eds., Josef Emler, Jan Gebauer, Jaroslav Goll (Prague: V komissí knihkupectví Edv. Valečky, 1893), 5:391–395.

5. Konstantin von Höfler, *Geschichtsschreiber der hussitischen Bewegung in Böhmen*, Fontes rerum Austriacarum 6 (Vienna: Aus der kaiserlich-königliche Hof- und Staatsdruckerei: 1865), 2:480.

6. Bartoš, *Manifesty města Prahy z doby husitské*, 275–278.

7. Ibid., 282–285.

8. Palacký, *Archiv český*, 227–228.

9. František Palacký, *Dějiny národu českého v Čechách a v Moravě* (Praha: Kvasnička & Hampl, 1939), 3:291–335. Bibliographical details for the reference works mentioned in the following footnotes were added (translator's note).

10. Václav Vladivoj Tomek, *Dějepis města Prahy* (Praha: W komissí u *Františka Řiwnáče*, 1879), 4:12–13, 25, 75, 84–85, 549, 580–587.

11. Friedrich von Bezold, *Zur Geschichte des Hussitentums: culturhistorische Studien* (München: Theodor Ackermann, 1874); *K dějinám husitství: kulturně historická studie*, trans. A. Chytil (Praha: J. Pelcl, 1904).

12. Ferdinand Hrejsa, *Dějiny křesťanství v Československu: Hus a husitství (Čechové v zápasu o ryzí křesťanství)* (Praha: HČEFB, 1947), 2:122–125.

13. František Dvorský, *Počátky kalicha a artikule pražské již l. 1417* (Praha: V komisi knihkupectví Fr. Řivnáče, 1907).

14. Václav Novotný, "Die Genesis der vier Prager Artikel. Von Mathilde Uhlirz. Wien Komm. Alf. Hölder, 1914. Str. 98. Sitzungsberichte der Kaiserlichen Akademie der Wissenschaften in Wien, Philosophisch-Historische Klasse 175 Bd., 3. Abhandlung" in *Časopis Matice moravské* 39 (1915): 287–298.

15. František Michálek Bartoš, *Do čtyř pražských artikulů: Z myšlenkových a ústavních zápasů let 1415–1420* (Prague: Nákladem Blahoslavovy společnosti, 1940).

16. Bartoš, *Manifesty města Prahy z doby husitské*, 275–278, 282–285.

17. Josef Pekař, *Žižka a jeho dob* (Praha: Odeon, 1992), 1:68–89, 214; 2:273; 3:59–74, 306–309, 330; 4:28, 48–57, 182–183.

The *Four Articles of Prague* (1420)

A New Translation on the Occasion of the 600th Anniversary of Their Declaration

TRANSLATED AND WITH NOTES BY
ANGELO SHAUN FRANKLIN

Preamble

To everyone in general and especially to every Christian, let it be solemnly known and announced that the Bohemian community and faithful Christians stand in divine hope, and with God's help—as far as they are possibly able with all of their possessions[1] and with their own life even unto death—intend to stand against all of those who are in opposition to this: establishing and legislating[2] nothing else other than these four Christian articles commanded by our Lord Jesus Christ in the New Testament.

The First Article

First: The word of God should be proclaimed[3] and preached throughout the Kingdom of Bohemia freely and without any impediments from Christian priests, just as our Savior commands: "Go into all the world and proclaim the gospel to the whole creation" (Matt 28:19; Mark 16:15). For according to Saint Paul, "the word of God is not bound" (2 Tim 2:9), but he says, "Pray that the word of God may spread quickly and be glorified"[4] (2 Thess 3:1). He also says, "I thank my God that I speak in the languages of all of you" (1 Cor 14:18) and "Do not forbid[5] speaking in other languages" (1 Cor 14:39), for Christ says, "Whatever I tell you in the darkness, speak in the light, and what you hear in your ear, speak or preach upon the housetops" (Matt. 10:27).

The Second Article

Second: The blessed sacrament of the body and blood of Christ should be given freely under both kinds to all faithful Christians who are not burdened with mortal sin, according to the institution and commandment of our Lord and Savior who says, "Take and eat, this is my body, and drink from it, all of you, for this is my blood of the new covenant, which is poured out for many" (Matt. 26:26–28; Mark 14:22–24; Luke 22:17–20); and here he commands his apostles, saying "Do this." And the interpretation of the *Glossa interlinearis* says, "In other words, take and give to others in remembrance of me."[6] And in John 6:53–56, the Savior binds all Christians to receive this sacrament under [penalty of committing] mortal sin, which is death of the soul, saying in this manner: "Truly, truly, I say to you, unless you eat the flesh of the Son of Man and drink his blood, you have no life in yourselves. Whoever eats my flesh and drinks my blood has eternal life . . . for my flesh is true food, and my blood is true drink. Whoever then eats my flesh and drinks my blood remains in me and I in him." Saint Paul also says in 1 Cor 1:28, "But let a person examine himself, then, and in this way let him eat of the bread and drink of the cup." However, since he means sacramental eating and drinking with your mouth, later in verse 29 he says, "For anyone who eats and drinks in an unworthy manner eats and drinks judgment on himself." Behold that in this verse when he says "in an unworthy manner" he means sacramental eating and drinking; for no one at all can eat and drink in an unworthy manner with his mouth except the one who he eats and drinks "in an unworthy manner" spiritually. And[7] in addition to this, there exist the laws and rules of the holy church in *De consecratione distinctione II: Conperimus.*[8] And the canon from the Council of Carthage (case 26 question 6: *Is qui*).[9] And Saint Gregory in his paschal sermon (*De consecratione distinctione II: Quid sit*).[10] And Saint Augustine in the same distinction *Dum hostia frangitur*[11] and also in the canon *Quia passus.*[12] And Saint Jerome when speaking of the prophet Zephaniah (case 1 question 1: *Sacerdotes*).[13] And Saint Dionysius in his book *De ecclesiastica hierarchia* (*The Ecclesiastical Hierarchy*) in the chapter on the Eucharist.[14] And Saint Cyprian the martyr in his Epistle 37 concerning the fallen ones (*de lapsis*).[15] And Saint Ambrose in *De consecratione distinctione II* on the sacraments.[16] And Origen in his sixteenth homily on Numbers.[17] And Saint Augustine in the first book of *De symbolo* (*A Sermon to Catechumens on the Creed*).[18] And in the quadragesimal sermon which begins with *Praedicaturus vobis* (*Since I am going to preach to you*) where he later on gives an example of the Manichean heretics who sometimes [participate in communion] only under the species of bread, but they refuse to drink the blood of God from the chalice.[19] And Fulgentius in his book *De divinis officiis* (*On the Divine Services*).[20] And Remigius on 1 Corinthians 10.[21] And

Saint Thomas Aquinas in *Super IV Sententiarum (Commentary on the Four Books of Sentences)* question 48,[22] and also part 3 question 76,[23] and question 73 article 2,[24] and question 82 article 3.[25] And Pope Innocent in his book on the sacraments especially in his final main point of chapter thirty-nine.[26] And Paschasius in his book on the sacraments in chapters ten, fourteen, and twenty.[27] And Lyra on the phrase "Come, eat my bread" in Prov. 9:5 and on 1 Cor 11:28.[28] And Guillelmus of Monte Lauduno in his *Sacramentale (Books on the Sacraments).*[29] And Albertus Magnus, Bishop of Regensburg, in his treatise on the office of the mass.[30] And there are many other saints and doctors who are witnesses to this article, whose writings have been included here for the sake of brevity; and whoever does not believe them can peruse their works.

The Third Article

Third: Since many priests and monks are exercising rights of civil dominion[31] over a great amount of material goods—violating the commandment of Christ, hindering their priestly office,[32] and causing great detriment to the lords of the secular estate—unlawful[33] dominion should be taken away and deprived of such priests in order that they can live according to the gospel and be brought back to the way of life[34] of Christ and the apostles. For it is written in the gospel: "And calling his twelve disciples, Christ sent them out, commanding them saying, 'Do not let silver or gold or money in your money-belts reign'"[35] (Matt. 10:9); and he says, "You know that the rulers of the Gentiles lord it over them, and those exercise authority over them call themselves 'benefactors.' But it must not be this way among you! But whoever is the greatest among you, let him be as the least, and whoever is a leader, let him be like a servant" (Matt. 20:25–27).[36] And he says the same elsewhere (Mark 10:42–44). In addition to this, Saint Peter says, "Not with domineering in the clerical order,[37] but for the purpose of being an example to the flock from the heart" (1 Pet 5:3). Saint Paul also says to Timothy, "Having food and clothing, we should be satisfied"[38] (1 Tim 6:8); and in 1 Cor 4:16 and in 11:1 where he says, "Be imitators of me, brothers, just as I also am of Christ." And "Pattern your lives after mine, and carefully observe those who walk according to the example you have in us" (Phil 3:17). And the apostolic way of life which Saint Peter followed was this: "Gold and silver do not belong to[39] me" (Acts 3:6). And the Scripture says, "The Lord said unto Aaron, 'You shall have no inheritance in their land, neither shall you have any portion among them'" (Num 18:20). The same is written in: Lev. 25:33; Num. 26:62; Deut. 10:9; 12:12; 14:27–29; 18:1; Josh. 13:14; 1 Chron. 6:[1–81]; Josh. 14:3; 18:7; 21:[1–23]. And the Lord God says, "This will be their inheritance: I am their inheritance. You are to give them no possession in Israel: I am their possession" (Ez 44:28). And Saint Paul says, "But you, O man of God, flee from these things" (1 Tim 6:11). For here the *Glossa ordinaria* says: "There is nothing so exasperating and so pernicious as when a man of the Church (and especially one who holds an eminent position) craves for the riches of this world, for such a man is a harmful nuisance not only to himself, but he is also presenting a contradictory example to others."[40] Therefore, Saint Paul says, "Flee from these things" (i.e., being rich and gaining temporal advantages). In addition to this, Saint Jerome, Saint Ambrose, and Saint Augustine—as is written in case 12 question 1 in the canon concerning clerics and in the following canons.[41] And from the third book in the title *De vita et honestate clericorum*[42] and in the chapter on brotherhood.[43] And Saint Bernard also wrote the same to Pope Eugenius.[44] And there are many other witnesses to this article from the Holy Scripture.

The Fourth Article

Fourth: All mortal sins and especially those sins committed publicly as well as other contemptible offenses against the law of God should be properly and reasonably prohibited and prevented[45] in each estate[46] by those who possess the authority to do so, in order that the ignoble reputation[47] afflicting the Kingdom of Bohemia and its language would be cleansed and its good name restored. Furthermore, as Saint Paul declares, it is not merely the one who commits these sins who is deserving of death, but also those who consent and enable others to commit them (Rom 1:32). Among the common people there exists the sins of fornication, gluttony, theft, murders, lies, deceit,[48] perjury, witchcraft, fraudulent and destructive[49] crafts and commerce, avarice, usury, and other evils similar to these; but among the clergy there exists the heresy of simony by extorting[50] money from baptism, from confirmation, from confessions, from the sacraments of holy communion and anointing with holy oil, from weddings, and charging fees for serving thirty masses[51] and other requiems, vigils, or other prayers purchased or reserved in advance on interest, for funerals, for singing or ringing bells in church, from the consecration of new priests, chapels, altars, cemeteries, for indulgences, for bishoprics and archbishoprics, provosts, the decanates, parishes, for every chaplaincy,[52] for exchanges,[53] for bulls and also other letters, and for all kinds of benefices and dignities and other spiritual things bought for any price at all, and other innumerable evils and heresies which derive from these are a heretical blight which defiles the holy church.[54] There are also other iniquities and sins such as pride, greed, adultery, concubinage and other impurities, wrath, envy, quarreling and dissensions, contentions, and indignant citations and frivolous lawsuits,[55] personal payments, offertories,[56] as well as money and other property gained for churches and buildings through hypocritical begging and by making false promises using pretentious[57] words to the simple-minded who are thereby extorted and victimized. Every faithful Christian is duty-bound to hate all of these sins even as he is obliged to hate their father (who is the devil himself),[58] and he should oppose, reprimand,[59] and prevent them in accordance to his calling.

CONCLUSION

Therefore, if anyone foists anything evil,[60] erroneous, shameful,[61] or immoral upon us either in writing or speaking, we plead and pray that such things would not be believed since that person is speaking lies[62] from malice and hatred as a false and spurious witness. For this is what we boldly confess before the Lord and before the whole world: that if God is willing, we will have no other intention in our hearts than to serve the Lord Jesus Christ and to commit ourselves[63] to him with all of our strength, energy, and possessions, and to practice and observe his law and commandments, as is appropriate for every good Christian, and to diligently abide by[64] these *four articles* which are founded upon[65] the commandments of God; and according to the law of God and his truth we must resist[66] all evil, adversity, and everyone who would coerce and drive us away from this good intention, and according to our calling we must protect ourselves against such violence by the secular arm. And if any kind of disturbance[67] happens by someone from among our multitude, we confess that it is not our desire, for if God is willing, we will stand against every mortal sin; and if anyone seems to be harmed by us, it will happen only in the case of dire necessity, since we must protect ourselves against the violence and cruelty[68] of God's enemies when it is according to the law of God. And above all, we confess that if it appears that any one of us has done anything wrong, we are ready and willing to make reparation and to wholeheartedly accept the message and the teachings of the Holy Scripture.

NOTES

1. Literally *goods* (symbolizing strength and resources).
2. In the sense of introducing, constituting, and issuing rules for people to follow, thus emphasizing the legal aspect of these four articles.
3. Literally *heralded*.
4. Or "enjoy unhindered progress, be illuminated, and be made famous."
5. This is probably a reference to reading and speaking in other languages in the context of some kind of ecclesiastical prohibition, either formally or informally based on the personal prerogative of individual priests. Jan Hus earlier mentioned

at least one example of this in a letter written to the people of Plzeň in 1411: "After writing this letter, another letter arrived in which it is written that priests are preventing people from reading the gospel in their native language of Czech or German. . . . And many of you know the truth and have learned that everyone can speak, confess, and if he is able even read the law of God in Latin (as Saint Mark wrote his gospel), in Greek (as Saint John composed his gospel and canonical epistles), in Hebrew (as Saint Matthew wrote his gospel), in Syriac (as Luke wrote his gospel), in Persian (as Saint Simon preached and wrote his gospel), in Aramaic (as Saint Bartholomew), and likewise in other languages. How then can you allow the priests to prevent people from reading the law of God in Czech or German?" *M. Jana Husi Korespondence a dokumenty,* ed. Václav Novotný (Praha: Nákladem komise pro vydávání pramenů náboženského hnutí českého, 1920), 106–107.

    6. *Glossa interlinearis* on Luke 22:19: "*Id est accipite et aliis date.*"

    7. Although it is not necessarily formal and sounds slightly redundant to begin every sentence with the word "and" in English, in this medieval Czech text the particular conjunction "and" (Czech *a*) is repeatedly used in incomplete sentences in order to emphasize a progressive development of the authorities cited, which ultimately leads up to the final claim that these authorities are in agreement with the testimony of the article itself, which was made on the basis of Scripture (i.e., Christ himself speaking in the gospels concerning communion with both bread and wine).

    8. *Corpus iuris canonici,* 1:1318 (D. 2 de cons. c. 12).

    9. *Corpus iuris canonici,* 1:1038 (C. 26 q. 6 c. 8). The is a reference to canon 76 of the Council of Carthage (436). See J.D. Mansi, *Sacrorum conciliorum nova et amplissima collectio,* 3:957.

    10. *Corpus iuris canonici,* 1:1343–1344 (D. 2 de cons. c. 73).

    11. *Corpus iuris canonici,* 1:1327 (D. 2 de cons. c. 37).

    12. *Corpus iuris canonici,* 1:1326 (D. 2 de cons. c. 36).

    13. *Corpus iuris canonici,* 1:391 (C. 1 q. 1 c. 90).

    14. *De Ecclesiastica Hierarchia in Patrologia Graeca,* 3:369–584 (col. 423–472 on the Eucharist); see 3.3.12 (col. 467–470). For the modern critical edition, see Günter Heil and Adolf M. Ritter, eds., *Pseudo-Dionysius Areopagita. De Coelesti Hierarchia, De Ecclesiastica Hierarchia, De Mystica Theologia, Epistulae,* Patristische Texte und Studien 67 2nd ed. (Berlin: De Gruyter, 2012), 61–132 (79–94 on the Eucharist, especially 92–93).

    15. Jan Hus made reference to Cyprian's letter as *Epistola 37 de lapsis* in his quaestio *De sanguine Christi sub specie vini a laicis sumendo.* See Matthias Flacius Illyricus, *Historia et monumenta Ioannis Hus atque Hieronymi Pragensis* (Nürnberg: Montanus and Neuberus, 1715), 1:53. See also Nicholas of Dresden's reference to Cyprian's *Epistola 37* in his *Collecta auctoritatum de materia sanguinis* (Prague, National Library of the Czech Republic MS IV.G.15. (Y.I.1.n.4.), fol. 228r). Their references are to Cyprian's synodical epistle to Pope Cornelius where he asked, "For how can we teach or challenge them to shed their blood for the confession of his name if we deny the blood of Christ to those who are going to fight? Or how can we make them fit for the chalice of martyrdom if we do not first allow them to participate deservedly in drinking the chalice of the Lord in the Church?" Cyprian, *Epistola*

synodica ad Cornelium de lapsis in Patrologia Latina, 3:851–862 (col. 856). See also Cyprian, *Epistulae in Corpus Scriptorum Ecclesiasticorum Latinorum: Epistula* 57.2 (3.2:651–652); *Epistula* 58.1 (3.2:656–657); *Epistula* 63.1–18 (3.2:701–716); see also *Liber de lapsis* 21 (3.2:253) and 25 (3.2:255).

16. *Corpus iuris canonici*, 1:1319 (D. 2 de cons. c. 14); 1:1348–1349 (D. 2 de cons. c. 83).

17. *Origenis in Numeros Homiliae in Patrologia Graeca*, 12:583–806; see Homily 16.9 (col. 701–702).

18. *De symbolo sermo ad catechumenos in Patrologia Latina*, 40:627–36; see 7.15 (col. 635–636).

19. Pope Leo I, *Sermones in Patrologia Latina*, 54:274–281; see 42.1 (col. 275) and 42.4–5 (col. 278–280). Pope Leo wrote, "They recoil at the mystery of human salvation and refuse to believe that Christ our Lord was truly born in the flesh in our actual nature, truly suffered, was truly buried, and was truly resurrected . . . however, when they conceal their unbelief by audaciously participating in our mysteries, they restrain themselves in the communion of the sacraments in order to hide themselves even more securely: they sometimes receive the body of Christ with an unworthy mouth, but they entirely refuse to drink the blood of our redemption" (col. 279–280). Augustine's explanation of the Manichaeans's refusal to drink blood is found in *De Haeresibus in Patrologia Latina*, 42:21–50; see chapter 46 (col. 34–38).

20. This is actually a reference to Rupert of Deutz's treatise *De divinis officiis* in *Patrologia Latina*, 170:11–333; see 2.9 (col. 40–41). Jakoubek of Stříbro cited Rupert as Fulgentius in his *Tractatus quod non solum sacerdotes: "Item Fulgencius De divinis officiis in libro, cuius prologus sic incipit: Ea, que per anni circulum"* (fol. 115v). For a collection of his related works, see *Tractatus Quod non solum sacerdotes (Auctoritates pro communione calicis ad populum laycalem, Tractatus de sanguine Domini nostri Iesu Cristi, Auctoritates sanctorum doctorum pro communione utriusque speciei, De communione* (Prague, National Library of the Czech Republic MS V.E.16. (fols. 112r–134r).

21. *Epistolam 1 ad Corinthios in Patrologia Latina*, 117:507–606 (col. 564). There remains some doubt concerning the actual authorship of certain works attributed to Haymon of Auxerre, Haymon Halberstadt, and Remigius of Auxerre. For a helpful explanation of the issues concerning authorship, see Sumi Shimahara, "Exégèse et politique dans l'œuvre d'Haymon d'Auxerre" in *Revue de l'histoire des religions*, 225 (2008/4): 471–486.

22. *Summa Theologiæ*, III Q. 48 A. 5 co; III Q. 48 A. 6 ad 2.

23. *Summa Theologiæ*, III. Q. 76 A. 2 ad 1.

24. *Summa Theologiæ*, III. Q. 73 A. 2 co.

25. *Summa Theologiæ*, III Q. 82 A. 3 ad 1.

26. *Mysteria evangelicae legis et sacramenti eucharistiae in Patrologia Latina*, 217:763–916; see *De sacro altaris mysterio*, 4.21 (col. 871–872); 4.39 (col. 881–882); 4.44 (col. 884–86).

27. *De corpore et sanguine domine in Patrologia Latina*, 120:1267–1350; see 10.1 (col. 1303–1306); 14.1–6 (col. 1316–1321); 15.3 (col. 1323–1324); 22.1–3 (col. 1330–1332).

28. Nicholas of Lyra, *Postilla literalis super totam Bibliam*: Proverbs 9:5: "*In utraque enim specie communicabant antiquitus fideles: sed propter periculum effusionis sanguinis ordinatum est, quod daretur laicis sub specie panis tantum*"; 1 Cor 11:28: "*accipit sub utraque specie.*"

29. Guillelmus of Monte Lauduno, *Sacramentale* (Prague, National Library of the Czech Republic MS V.B.17. (Y.II.1.n.43.), fols. 224r–297r); see fol. 259: "*recipiendo corpus totam veritatem accipit, licet non totum sacramentum.*" "*Ideo in multis locis communicatur cum pane et vino, id est cum toto sacramento.*"

30. *Liber de sacramento Eucharistæ* in *Alberti Magni Opera Omnia*, eds. Auguste and Emile Borgnet (Paris: Vivès 1899), 38:191–463; see 3.1.3.3. (245–246); 3.2.1.1: "*Super triticum et vinum ruminabunt; hec enim duo ab omnium fidelium ore ruminanda frequentata memoria sunt in sacramento, qui hec duo maximum fidelium bonum sunt in misterio posita*" (280–281); 3.2.5.1–6 (297–304); 6.2.1.1–4 (364–368).

31. That is, they feel they are entitled to rule or dominate over goods according to the principle of civil dominion, with dominion involving both possessions and authority.

32. This is a play on words since *office* was a virtual synonym for authority, and they were specifically abusing their official authority as priests.

33. That is, unjust, unauthorized, or unwarranted by the law of God, thus illegitimate.

34. Or *estate*.

35. That is, do not let money wield power over you and dominate you.

36. This Scripture passage is cited according to the gospel account of Luke 22:25–27.

37. This is according to the text of the Latin Vulgate: "*neque ut dominantes in cleris, sed forma facti gregis ex animo.*" The Knox translation reads "not tyrannizing, each in his own sphere, but setting an example, as best you may, to the flock."

38. Literally *we have enough.*

39. This a play on words since the Czech word means *does not belong, has no right*, or *is not proper or suitable for someone.* The underlying meaning is: "I have no claim to gold and silver, because it is not proper or suitable for me to demand such a right."

40. *Patrologia Latina*, 114:632: "*Nihil enim tam asperum tamque perniciosum, quam si vir ecclesiasticus maxime qui sublimem tenet locum divitiis huius seculi studeat, quia non solum sibi ipsi, sed et ceteris obest quibus contrariam dat formam.*" This gloss from the *Glossa Ordinaria* was copied from Ambrosiaster's *In epistolam beati Pauli ad Timothem primam* in *Patrologia Latina*, 17:487–512; see 6.9–10 (col. 509).

41. *Corpus iuris canonici*, 1:675–681 (C. 12. q. 1. c. 1–12).

42. *Corpus iuris canonici*, 2:449–454 (X 3.1.1–16).

43. *Corpus iuris canonici*, 2:533 (X 3.24.2).

44. *De consideratione libri quinque ad Eugenium tertium* in *Patrologia Latina*, 182: 727–808; see 2.6.11 (col. 748).

45. Literally *thwarted.*

46. That is, regardless of one's social status.

47. Literally a "crooked" reputation. This phrase could also be rendered as "slanderous rumors."

48. Guile, duplicity, or deception.

49. Pernicious, harmful, or destructive.

50. Or exacting (demanding and obtaining) a payment. This is a sarcastic play on words, since priests conveniently "acquired money from services" in a way which ingeniously "extorted it from people" for some particular service. It literally means to "force something out of someone."

51. There was a long-standing ancient custom of offering a series of masses for thirty consecutive days immediately after someone's death in order to release their soul from the punishments of purgatory. They are called Gregorian masses after Pope Gregory I who initiated the tradition. Gregory's own personal account of the incident is found in his *Dialogues*. Gregory, *Dialogorum libri quatuor* in *Patrologia Latina*, 77:149–430; see 4.55 (col. 416–421).

52. That is, the office of an altarist, altar-thane, or chaplain who is entrusted with the liturgical services at one designated altar. The revenue reserved for the chaplain gained from offerings or donations made on the altar is called altarage (Latin *altaragium*), although it is more commonly known as stole-fee, honorarium, or stipend.

53. This word connotes both exchanges and substitutes. It was a common practice in Bohemia at the time to exchange and rent out parishes to someone else who would serve as a substitute priest or to secure a parish and then rent it in order to gain continual revenue. For example, see *Magister Iohannes Hus Opera Omnia*, 4:226: "And when they are able to acquire a parish, they usually rent it according to the municipal law, thus securing for themselves a constant stream of income. And so in this way simony continues for a long time due to both parties: for they receive revenue without labor"; 4:242: "Furthermore, I will mention the underhanded craftiness running rampant in the swapping of parishes and renting them in exchange. Since again they are continually purchasing the care of souls from every church, who can excuse of them of this sin? Since a priest also rents the church to another and then cavorts around in town without laboring at all, while in the meantime the renter rigorously shears and milks the sheep."

54. Similar sins related to the heresy of simony were mentioned by Jan Hus in his Czech treatise *Svatokupectví (On Simony)*. *Magister Iohannes Hus Opera Omnia*, 4:202: "for confession, for baptism, for anointing with holy oil, for serving mass, for funerals, for the consecration of a church, an altar, a chalice, or a cope, for the confirmation of benefices"; 215, 218, 234–237: "from baptism, from confession, from funerals, from the Eucharist, from anointing with holy oil, from marriage ceremonies, from thirty masses"; 244: "bishoprics, provosts, or parishes, canonries"; passim.

55. These summons or citations (Latin *citationes*) were a part of the process of legal action undertaken in order to bring someone to justice according to the Bohemian provincial law from the eleventh to the seventeenth century. See Karel Malý et al., *Dějiny českého a československého práva do roku 1945*, 4th ed. (Praha: Leges, 2010), 47, 99–101, 118–119. The critique here is aimed at the petulant and irascible behavior evidenced in resentfully "dragging" someone else to court over trifling matters.

56. Or personal gifts or "sacrificial offerings" used for ecclesiastical purposes.

57. In the sense of being the epitome of sacrilegious pretentiousness.

58. See John 8:44 and 1 John 3:8.

59. That is, to rebuke and to hold in check.

60. Or *egregious* (from the Latin *egregius*: literally "standing out from the flock").

61. Disgraceful or scandalous.

62. Literally *untruth*.

63. That is, to make a pledge or promise to someone in dedication or devotion.

64. *To stand for, support, and remain loyal to these articles* or *to insist upon and adhere to these articles.*

65. That is, *hinge upon* or *are dependent upon.*

66. Be in opposition to, protest, and resist.

67. Or *disorder.*

68. Or *tyranny.*

Part II

THE *FOUR ARTICLES OF PRAGUE* WITHIN THE PUBLIC SPHERE OF HUSSITE BOHEMIA

Introduction

The periodization of the Hussite movement has been the subject of many historical works in the past, and its individual epochs have been explored and analyzed from various perspectives. In essence, it can be considered as an established fact that the main events of the Hussite movement which occurred between 1419 and 1434 were preceded by a long period of other events which prepared for later monumental changes. The primary aim of this work, however, is not to examine in strict detail the specific causes behind those changes nor the general characteristics of the Hussite era. The publications of František Bartoš (1889–1972),[1] František Šmahel,[2] Petr Čornej,[3] and especially the extensive and dynamic work written by Howard Kaminsky (1924–2014)[4] should be consulted as valuable references. Instead, our predominant aim here is to evaluate the entire Hussite movement from the perspective of both the state and the law (i.e., its legal and political roots and ramifications). The Czech legal historian Václav Vaněček (1905–1985) in particular provided an excellent qualified analysis of the legal history of the era, and even if his conclusions are at least partially ideologically influenced, they are nonetheless cogent.[5] In his cumulative work, he expressed the legitimate idea that the state apparatus in the pre-Hussite period remained virtually unchanged since its establishment during the reign of Emperor and King Charles IV (1316–1378).

The often quite heated legal discussions were usually concerned with matters which had little significance in regard to the state system of organization. One of these themes dealt with peasant escheats (i.e., who would receive an inheritance from a peasant) or a specific priestly escheat. Master Vojtěch Raňkův of Ježova (1320–1388)—professor at Charles University, former rector of the Sorbonne, and the one who preached a sermon at the emperor's funeral and called him *pater patriae* ("father of the fatherland")—was particularly concerned with the topic.[6]

Despite the rather weak reign of Václav IV from 1378 to 1419, the structures of the state remained intact. Vaněček correctly noted that this was quite apparent in the work of Hus's stalwart defender and companion Jan of Jesenice (d. 1420).[7] In his words, with the explosion of the Hussite Revolution, the state apparatus practically ceased to function and exist. At the time, however, Vaněček stated that the impulses for a new organization of the state proceeded from the lower social classes (i.e., the burghers and the lower nobility); however, this cannot be surmised to represent the entire truth.

While the classes previously mentioned by Vaněček played a major role, it is also important to inquire as to the exact foundation upon which their ideas were based. Ideas such as "a revolutionary explosion of the popular masses," or the idea proposed by Josef Macek (1922–1991) that the revolutionary model of Tábor was a community of consumerists instead of the manufacturers of communism, are hardly sufficient explanations.[8] The issue is much more complex and requires more in-depth historical, philosophical, and theological analyses to properly understand the legal situation.

Of course, Vaněček is correct in his view that following 1434, an era of "normalization" began in which law and order were being restored. Although he interpreted it as a form of counterrevolution, he was not mistaken in his conclusion concerning that period:

> Law and order were restored in the state, old political and legal institutions were revived, and the feudal state apparatus began to function even under the leadership of King Sigismund (1368–1437), who was once declared an enemy of the state and its nation (i.e., people). But in fact such events had been the case for many years, and the revolutionary content could not be erased from the history of the country, the distribution of property within the lands, the economy, the political structures, or even from the minds of the inhabitants themselves. There was simply no going back to the way things had been before. The results of the revolution were apparent, making it necessary to respect and deal with them even to the point of enshrining them within the law itself. The Hussite movement has left a permanent mark of its rule on the Czech people.[9]

Although the terminology employed is clearly Marxist, the conclusions are objective and accurate, for without the Hussite movement the following developments would not have been possible: the appointment of the highest provincial officials by the lower class nobility, the election of Jiří of Poděbrady (1420–1471) as king, and later the relative freedom of religion which was unheard of in other countries at that time (e.g., the *Religious Peace of Kutná Hora* in 1485).

While acknowledging Hus's contribution, Vaněček definitely avoided the plausible role of Master Jan Hus (1371–1415) and his impact upon the entire era. Instead, he saw the decisive period of the Hussite Revolution as the consequence of a slowly maturing revolutionary process. Although this fits conveniently with his personal worldview, as any expert of his stature is, he must have been aware of the important and influential role which predominant personalities have played in history. Regardless, the creation of the *Four Articles of Prague*—which, in their modified form, governed life within the Kingdom of Bohemia up until 1620—was one of the most important aspects of the revolution. It is for this express reason that this work will focus not merely on Hus's legal arguments, but also on the actual articles themselves—the circumstances surrounding their origin, their specific content, their effects, and how renowned legal historians have reacted to them as a legal document. Proper attention will also be given to the major issue of their continuing influence on the legal history of the Bohemian state (e.g., in the Compacts of Basel in 1436).

Their unilateral abolition by Pope Pius II (1405–1464) did nothing to change the fact that their legacy continued to endure in the Lands of the Bohemian Crown.[10] This extended far beyond the laity receiving the chalice, although this particular feature was the most visible and probably that which caused the greatest aggravation of the Catholic Church against the Hussite movement. The transformation of the monarchy into a monarchy of the Estates in the second half of the fifteenth century and throughout the entire sixteenth century had its direct roots in the Hussite movement. Of course, one cannot forget the vast amounts of literature dedicated to Hussite movement from the times of František Palacký (1798–1876). His expertise and appraisal will remain in the background of this work, which cannot possibly reflect upon every minor aspect of the movement. The main sources employed will be the works of the Czech legal historians Jiří Kejř (1921–2015),[11] Karel Malý,[12] Václav Vaněček, and several others, including primary literary sources (i.e., the actual *Four Articles*, chronicles, annals, etc.) drawn from the Hussite era. Despite certain reservations and due caution concerning their particular formulations, their conclusions remain clear and convincing.

NOTES

1. František Michálek Bartoš, *Husitská revoluce: Doba Žižkova 1415–1426*, vol. 1 (Prague: Československé akademie věd, 1965); *Husitská revoluce: Vláda bratrstev a její pád 1426–1437*, vol. 2 (Prague: Academia, 1966).
2. František Šmahel, *Husitská revoluce*, 4 vols. (Prague: Historický ústav Akademie věd České republiky, 1993).

3. Petr Čornej, *Velké dějiny zemí koruny české*, vol. 5 (Prague/Litomyšl: Paseka, 2000); Petr Čornej and Milena Bártlová, *Velké dějiny zemí koruny české*, vol. 6 (Prague/Litomyšl: Paseka, 2007); Petr Čornej, *Světla a stíny husitství (události, osobnosti, texty, tradice): výbor z úvah a studií* (Prague: Nakladatelství Lidové noviny, 2011).

4. Howard Kaminsky, *A History of the Hussite Revolution*. This work of outstanding scholarship includes an insightful analysis of the sociological and legal aspects of the Hussite Revolution.

5. Václav Vaněček, *Dějiny státu a práva v Československu do roku 1945: vysokoškolská učebnice* (Prague: Orbis, 1976).

6. See Jaroslav Kadlec, *Mistr Vojtěch Raňkův z Ježova* (Prague: Univerzita Karlova, 1969); for the Latin text of his speech, see *Fontes Rerum Bohemicarum*, eds. Jaroslav Goll et al. (Prague: Nákladem nadání Františka Palackého, 1882), 3:433–441.

7. Vaněček, *Dějiny státu a práva v Československu*, 126. For a helpful monograph on Jesenice, see Jiří Kejř, *Husitský právník M. Jan z Jesenice* (Prague: Nakladatelství Československé akademie věd, 1965).

8. Josef Macek, *Husitské revoluční hnutí* (Praha: Rovnost, 1952); 76–94; *Tábor v husitském revolučním hnutí*, vol. 1 (Prague: Nakladatelství Československé akademie věd, 1956), 11–41.

9. Vaněček, *Dějiny státu a práva v Československu*, 126.

10. Pope Pius II (Enea Silvio Bartolomeo Piccolomini) also authored a work examining ancient Bohemian history titled *Historia Bohemica*. For a Latin edition paired with a Czech translation, see Enea Silvio, *Historia Bohemica (Historie česká)*, trans. Dana Martinková, Alena Hadravová, and Jiří Matl (Prague: Koniasch Latin Press, 1998).

11. Jiří Kejř, *Husův proces* (Prague: Vyšehrad, 2000); *Husovo odvolání od soudu papežova k soudu Kristovu* (Ústí nad Labem: Albis International, 1999); Jiří Kejř, *Husité* (Prague: Panorama, 1984); Jiří Kejř, "Jan Hus jako právní myslitel," in Jan Blahoslav Lášek, ed., *Jan Hus mezi epochami, národy a konfesemi: sborník z mezinárodního sympozia, konaného 22.–26. září 1993 v Bayreuthu, SRN* (Prague: Česká křesťanská akademie, 1995), 197–207. The original German version is "Johannes Hus als Rechtsdenker," in *Jan Hus—Zwischen Zeiten, Völkern, Konfessionen: Vorträge des internationalen Symposions in Bayreuth vom 22. bis 26. September 1993*, Ferdinand Seibt et al., eds (Munich: R. Oldenbourg, 1997), 213–226.

12. Karel Malý, *Trestní právo v Čechách v 15.–16. století* (Prague: Univerzita Karlova, 1979); Karel Malý, "K právnímu odkazu husitství," in Jan Blahoslav Lášek, ed., *Jan Hus mezi epochami, národy a konfesemi: sborník z mezinárodního sympozia, konaného 22.–26. září 1993 v Bayreuthu, SRN* (Prague: Česká křesťanská akademie, 1995), 208–212. The original German version is "Die Bibel und das hussitische Rechtsdenken," in *Jan Hus—Zwischen Zeiten, Völkern, Konfessionen*, 227–234.

Chapter 1

Master Jan Hus and His Predecessors

There was never really any initiative from a legal perspective from Hus's so-called predecessors; although they often criticized the social conditions, inspiring figures such as Konrád Waldhauser (c. 1326–1369) and Jan Milíč of Kroměříž (c. 1320–1374) had called for an inner conversion, while Matěj of Janov (c. 1350–1393) encouraged frequent communion for the laity.[1] Nevertheless, if one were to search for anything which would foreshadow or lead to the future Hussite reforms, an answer could be found in the writings of Master Vojtěch Raňkův of Ježova.[2] During extremely disturbing times of church schism, he postulated in a very careful and polemical manner that if two schismatic popes exist at the same time, then the head of the church must be none other than Jesus Christ himself. Perhaps this alone could be construed as a significant legal testimony, concerned primarily with ecclesiastical law but also having consequences in the realm of secular law. Jiří Kejř wrote in great detail concerning the legal legacy of Master Jan Hus throughout several different publications. Since it is clear that the later formulation of the *Four Articles of Prague* was ideologically based on Hus's own work, it is necessary to state Kejř's primary theses and offer some insightful remarks.

Kejř was well aware that it is simply not possible to present Hus as a lawyer who contributed to the development of legal sciences in any significant or definitive way. Based on the sources available, Johannes Cochlaeus (1479–1552) stated that Hus was nonetheless highly knowledgeable of the law and legal matters. It might even appear to some that Hus's trial before the papal court (which lasted several years) motivated his interest in law. Kejř refuted that notion, stating that "the inner development of his reformatory efforts led him into an increasingly intense conflict with the established and long-standing system of ecclesiastical organization and authority, which was impossible without an inevitable and radical confrontation with the valid legal order (i.e., the applicable rule of law)."³

Although this was not his original aim, Hus eventually fully rejected ecclesiastical law as a human invention and demanded evidence from Scripture. Kejř explained that among the specific legal sources which Hus had available, the *Decretum Gratiani* remained his primary source since Hus quoted it in all of his major works; and while they are mentioned less frequently in his writings than the *Decretum Gratiani*, Hus was intimately knowledgeable of the following collections of canon law: *Decretales Gregorii IX (Liber Extra)*, *Liber Sextus (Sixth Book of the Credentials)*, and *Constitutiones Clementinae (Liber Septimus)*.⁴ He was also familiar with edicts and sources dispersed later such as the papal bull *Unam Sanctam* by Boniface VIII and the constitution of Benedict XI entitled *Sancta Romana Ecclesia*.⁵

He also used a collection of glosses on the *Decretum Gratiani,* entitled the *Glossa Ordinaria*.⁶ Hus did not investigate the origin of the manuscripts he used, as such a scientific activity was not customary at all in his time. This explains why the *Glossa Ordinaria* was cited as Johannes Teutonicus (since it was in many manuscripts and also later in the incunabula), despite the text actually being an updated version from Bartholomew of Brescia (1200–1258).⁷ Kejř also listed additional legal writings used by Hus, but they bear relatively little significance for the purposes of this work. Those sources include Archidiaconus (*Rosarium Guidona de Baysio*), a commentary on *Liber Sextus* from the same author, Henricus de Segusia-Hostiensis (1200–1271), Gottfredus de Trano, Innocentius, Iohannes Andreae, Guillaume Durand (1230–1296), and others. In some of his polemical works, Hus refers to the writings of Dina del Mugello and to Roman law (*De libris hereticorum legendis*).⁸ Kejř assumes that this might be at least partially due to Master Jan of Jesenice, who was Hus's legal advisor on matters of Roman law.

Surprisingly, Hus himself specifically addressed the topic of escheats in one of his letters addressed to an unnamed recipient where he warned against the abuse of this feudal right.⁹ He repeatedly rejected usury. As someone who was familiar with corrupt and unjust judicial practices, he demanded just sentences and verdicts. This can be seen in his major *Exposition of the Ten Commandments*, which contains deliberations on legal and criminal matters.¹⁰ He did not cite exactly from his sources, because the laws which he was considering were in part customary or consuetudinary law, so he had no recourse to the available sources anyway. Additionally, Hus was very critical of how judicial processes were enforced by the judicial authorities and regarded them as incorporating a clearly unjust set of practices.

Since Hus was primarily a theologian above all else, one might pose the question concerning his rationale for working with legal sources so frequently. Kejř proposed that "Hus often reached for legal sources not in order to argue their legal authority but rather to support his conclusions with their theological faithfulness."[11] Theological perspective, moral substance, and ethical evaluation constituted the authoritative and decisive criteria for Hus. According to Kejř, this was a return to the original content of the *Decretum Gratiani*. Hus was assisted by

> several features of canon law, in whose institutions both the legal and theological aspects were merged and pervaded each other. There are many questions in which both of these disciplines must be taken into consideration when examining any internal content and evaluating the ability to predicate historical realities. The boundaries between a criminal act and a sin, jurisdiction and the magisterium, marriage as a legal relationship and as a sacrament, or between the role of a cleric as an administrator of property values and as a spiritual advisor were not strictly defined.[12]

Practically, the canon law, councils, doctors and edicts functioned in terms of authority as being based on divine revelation and thus stood on the same level as Scripture. Scholastic literature remained firmly rooted within the church, and even when it had to concern itself with legal institutions, it considered them to be self-evident, necessary, and just. Hus, of course, adhered to a different conviction, which explains to some extent why he deviated from the *status quo* and became a martyr for the truth (cf. figure 1.1).

Kejř emphasized that in matters of law (as well as in other disciplines) the key figure for both Hus and for many other Hussite scholars was John Wyclif (c. 1330–1384; see figure 1.2). However, this fact does not mean that Hus's legal (as well as his philosophical and theological) ideas were identical; Hus was not a mere epigone of Wyclif. Whereas Wyclif was characterized by juridical criticism, Hus on the other hand was defined by moral enthusiasm. Moreover, Hus was extremely cautious in his reception of Wyclif's ideals and did not adopt his more radical ideas. For Hus, the dogmatic and normative character of his sources did not carry as great an importance as did their moral and ethical value. In the all-too-common conflict of morality versus law which is often present in various legal systems, morality maintained the absolute priority for Hus while the authority of the law in itself was not decisive. He invoked the law "not as a sufficient standard but rather used it as evidence and proof for his legal theses, which were derived from theological and ethical presuppositions."[13] Legal regulations lost their normative character as far as Hus was concerned, which meant that they were not a source of divine revelation.

This was a major legal breakthrough, since from a moral standpoint Hus was led to challenge decisions which were formally in accordance with the law (i.e., denying an unjust excommunication), a practice which was in

Figure 1.1   The Oldest Depiction of Master Jan Hus on the Pyre in the So-Called Martinice Bible around 1430. *Source*: Prague: Library of the Academy of Sciences of the Czech Republic, MS no sig. fol. 11v. Credit: Jan Blahoslav Lášek

full conformity with the law. Kejř quite correctly postulated the foundation underlying Hus's approach which would inevitably cause him to come into a ruptured relationship with the Roman Church: the basis for his legal standpoint essentially advocated reform—completely and beyond all discussion. "It is the law of God that is seen as the preferential, supreme, and perfect norm which contains all other norms within itself and thus cannot be replaced or exchanged with anything else. The law of God is the decisive criteria for all moral and legal aspects of life and determines the validity of human laws, which must never stand in opposition to the law of God."[14]

Figure 1.2   Wyclif, Hus, and Luther in the Malostranský Graduál (Lesser Town of Prague Gradual) from 1572. *Source*: National Library in Prague, MS XVII A3, fol. 363r. Credit: Jan Blahoslav Lášek

Hus did not reject all human laws in any capacity whatsoever; he rejected those laws which were in violation of the divine law present in Scripture, since he considered those laws to be invalid. According to Hus, the law of God is contained in Scripture, and therefore Scripture is sufficient for governing human society.[15] In Kejř's interpretation he did not perceive Hus as being dogmatic, since Hus admitted as much that some commandments could be lessened to a certain degree. In one *quaestio* concerning the law, Hus affirmed a distinction between imperative commands and admonishing exhortations, although no such distinction is made in his subsequent writings.[16] A small treatise where this concept is evidenced in a very unambiguous way is *De sufficiencia legis Christi* (*On the Sufficiency of the Law of Christ*).[17] The legal approach Hus wanted to defend before the Council of Constance is clearly declared in this treatise, and although it bears the notable influence of Wyclif,[18] the resulting work undoubtedly represents Hus's original contribution.

Kejř made a proper assessment in his view that the main idea of divine law being the exclusive and binding obligatory force would certainly be in direct contradiction of law as it was understood at that time. Therefore, when Hus stated from the very outset that his desire was to entrust the decision regarding his dispute to divine law, it was akin to throwing down the gauntlet; his own words made it patently clear that he did not respect the authority of either the court or the church itself. Considering his era, this was a truly revolutionary act indeed. For clarification, Hus certainly was not a legal nihilist at all; however, in Hus's particular conception, when observed from the perspective of the divine law, the human legal order loses its highest organizational order for regulating human society. Hus was convinced that people needed a set of binding norms for living in order for the mutual coexistence of common life to benefit everyone. But these norms should not be created "via human means and influenced by human interests."[19] Only the divine law of God was to possess the decisive and ultimate binding authority and obligatory power.

Such a legal concept is highly exceptional, since in theory it could be used to reject any and all secular and ecclesiastical norms. Kejř labeled this concept as the "legal-theological"[20] approach to law and justice. This was an important question for Hus and his contemporaries but also for those who immediately survived him: what is the law of God? Originally this question was to be the subject matter of the disputations (*quodlibet*) which Hus led.[21] The major *quaestio* came from Jakoubek of Stříbro (1372–1429), who most certainly formulated his own answer after consulting and agreeing with Master Jan Hus. After all, Hus's own corpus contains the term "law of God" quite frequently, and as Kejř aptly added, "It is not necessary to emphasize that all of the divergent reflections concern the divine law (even if they show certain nuances of meaning in different contexts), since they ultimately always lead to the same result, that is, a clarification of the central category of Hus's argumentation and that of Hussite legal thought in general."[22]

Since it provides a significant and interesting backdrop for our theme, it is necessary to present Hus's own conception and evaluation of the human legal order. As Hus would express it, the human legal order has neither the authority nor the power to properly function alone by itself. When judging the human legal order, the all-important category for Hus was justice, which of course he considered to be derived from the law of God. Hus did not formally renounce Aristotle; in fact, he cited him quite often and made frequent reference to Aristotle's distinction of justice in relation to divine power and the righteousness of God.[23]

Outside of a theological perspective, the most appropriate terms which adequately describe Hus's approach are *moral* and *subjective*. Hus was mindful and aware from his own personal experience that the concept of justice could become distorted or perverted; for example, while an act or decision before a court might be technically in order according to the law, it could simultaneously be in complete violation of that which is just in the eyes of the Lord. For him, the only true justice is that justice which exists before God, and this alone should be used as the standard for measuring human relationships. That which merely impersonates justice in appearance is actually fictitious justice and a human invention guided by evil intentions.

Following the apostle Paul, Hus proclaimed that only those who were "just" before the Lord would live (Rom. 1:17; Gal. 3:11). As a result, justice is a prevalent topic in Hus's writings, with the primary criteria being neither mankind nor their human institutions but the will of God, since nothing is possible without a connection to justice and the law of God. "The connection between divine law and justice allowed Hus to consider justice as a concrete concept, through which the highest norm is projected into real legal life. That is why justice is not a mere ethical postulate, but is transformed into a strictly definite criterion for applying the law in each individual case."[24]

It should come as no surprise that everyone at his trial in Constance was astounded by his words; after all, Hus did not embrace the law as it was understood at the time as a binding category. As Kejř pointed out, Hus's stance did not prevent him from using the established terminology present within the law at that time (e.g., in his interpretation of Peter Lombard's views on marriage laws within the *Four Books of Sentences*).[25] In this particular case, it was not so difficult of a task for Hus to comply because he was willing and able to acknowledge marriage laws considered from their moral aspects. If he had directly challenged the standards of the legal order in his interpretation of Lombard's *Sentences*, it would have been precluded and discredited. Despite that, Kejř noted that Hus's commentary clearly exhibits the tell-tale signs of a theologian and not a lawyer.

The conclusion that Hus was familiar with the legal institutions and their terminology is supported by the evidence that some of his sermons or treatises included known legal terms used in a precise and unmistakable manner. Hus's approach always remained subjective, however, since he advocated the law of God to reign above all else. Kejř maintained that Master Hus was at fault for the unfortunate outcome of his trial, since he refused to accept that the formal procedures of the trial had to be followed, regardless of his own personal disagreement. For Hus, the law was an abstract norm while the rights and the application of laws were associated with people—that is, lawyers. In fact, one of the reasons why he opposed the church as a legal institution was due to his long-standing concern that the church had appointed too many lawyers into positions of leadership. Hus desired that even the pope should be first and foremost a theologian.

The entire tragedy of Hus's case is displayed in his "revolutionary" act on October 18, 1412: when an interdict was placed upon him, he appealed to Jesus Christ as the supreme judge. A plethora of literature has already been written on this subject, and all accounts essentially emphasize Hus's appeal to "the most righteous Judge who knows, defends and judges, perfectly upholds and rewards the just cause of every man."[26] Considered from the perspective of legal theory, this was an appeal which reflected his conviction; according to the regulations of that time, he went against the formally well-known verdict and appealed to an improper institution which was not acknowledged by canon law. This is the rationale undergirding the specific terminology Hus employed in his appeal.

Whether viewed from a theological or a psychological perspective, in either case, that which led him to make such a decision can be understood as a rigorous and consistent defense of his personal convictions. As Kejř points out again,

> In his mind, the official Church and the ecclesiastical court were incapable of finding true justice. The appeal and its later defense represent the pinnacle of Hus's legal teachings, where the unambiguous superiority of Jesus Christ above secular authority became crystal clear, because he is both the supreme lawgiver and the supreme judge. In any case, it was through his appeal that Hus also demonstrated his confidence concerning his unjust excommunication.[27]

So what kind of influence did this courageous yet totally futile attempt have on future legal efforts? It played an absolutely decisive role, for it already represents a modern approach: no matter how fair or unjust they were, formal regulations no longer held the same authority as before, but conscience instead became determinative. It was Hus's conscience which allowed him to stand against the unjust structure of society, because he no longer deemed it to be following or obeying the law of God.

Hus was also preoccupied with several issues which overlapped with legal affairs: ecclesiastical administration and its power within the church, secular power and privileges of the clergy, the papacy, church assets (i.e., wealth), and the relationship between church and state. Unfortunately, there is no monograph dedicated to interpreting Hus's perspectives and opinions on secular law and jurisprudence. Most available publications tend to reflect his ecclesiastical-legal opinions, though one should not forget that secular and ecclesiastical laws in those times enjoyed a rather mutually close relation.

Although since he was not a theologian, Jiří Kejř was not fully able to understand Hus from a theological viewpoint, Kejř was certainly correct in one aspect: from an external perspective, Hus's teachings were (aside from ecclesiology) fairly orthodox and contained only a few real deviations from church dogma. The extensive writings of Vlastimil Kybal (1880–1958)[28] and Paul de Vooght (1900–1983)[29] prove as much. However, both his conception of the church itself and his view of justice are neither standard nor orthodox. Hus conceived of the church not as a hierarchical organization but rather as a fellowship of elect and reconciled sinners. His distinct views had ecclesiastical-political consequences and signified a challenge to the church and the society at the time. The teachings of Hus relativized what was previously seen as the established social bonds and represented a serious threat to the hierarchical church, its privileged position in society, and its claims for secular dominion. It is no wonder, then, that in later programs seeking to achieve social and ecclesiastical reforms, we find demands such as jurisdiction of secular power over those members of the clergy who had committed a criminal offense, or a radical demand to forbid the church from wielding power in secular affairs (e.g., the *Four Articles of Prague*).

From a formal perspective, Hus's reflections were still rooted in canon law and were explicitly conservative in their terminology. On the other hand,

> they were already searching for ways to leave the ground of valid medieval law, and thus in their ideological content led to the future Reformation. Ethical categories (e.g., the emphasis on justice or the exclusive and irreversibly binding power of the law of God over the validity of secular ones—which by its very foundation negates the authority of the church)—signify an almost total denial of the established legal order.[30]

In so doing, Hus established a criterion which foreign and unknown to canon law.

Out of all the theologians who were influenced by Hus's writings, Master Jakoubek of Stříbro was among the most prominent. Although he was a theologian, he was also concerned with legal matters and wrote a tract against usury (*Contra Usuram*).[31] Following Hus's legal principle of the sufficiency of the law of Christ, he attempted to apply that principle (*lex Christi*) in all of his subsequent theological proceedings.[32] The previously mentioned Jan of Jesenice (a lawyer by profession) was another individual who defended Hus's principles and whose commitment contributed to his infamous death in prison around 1420 due to the machinations of Oldřich II of Rožmberk (1403–1462).

The period following Hus's death is of utmost importance since it demonstrated that the master's execution had done nothing at all to extinguish rebellion in Bohemia. The chalice was at the center of the entire conflict; and while it was primarily a theological issue, it also represented an important legal concern. While it is well known that Hus himself did not serve

communion to the laity from the chalice, according to a later testimony from
Jan Rokycana (1396–1471), Hus fully endorsed the practice when he wrote to
Master Jakoubek during his time in prison in 1414.[33] Although Hus initially
urged him to wait on implementing such practices until he had returned from
Constance, Jakoubek did not wait for Hus and started serving communion
under both kinds (*sub utraque specie*) to the laity, since it was already apparent that Hus would never return again.[34]

The issue surrounding the chalice was always a matter of power and was
not at all something to be questioned. Even though the council admitted that
communion under both kinds for the laity had previously been practiced for
centuries, this acknowledgment did not prevent them from officially prohibit-
ing the chalice on June 15, 1415.[35] Their prohibition ultimately changed nothing, as the practice spread in the lands of the Bohemian Crown like wildfire
and separated Hus's supporters from the rest of society. Other interesting
facts associated with these events which were connected to nationality will
be explained later in chapters 4 and 5.

The protest congress of Bohemian nobility led by Lacek of Kravař (c.
1348–1416) had a significant legal impact on further development, since
previously such congresses were held separately in Bohemia and in Moravia,
and usually with some underlying practical purpose. This congress, however,
took place in Prague with the full attendance of the higher nobility from all
three of the Crown lands: Bohemia, Moravia, and Silesia. A defense league
of armed forces was organized in September 1415 and lasted for six years.
This league would advance to become one of the foundations of the future
Estates. The congress "adopted Hus as their own" and immediately took
decisive action. The ensuing accusations of heresy by both the Kingdom of
Bohemia and the Margraviate of Moravia were deemed as dubious and false,
and they unequivocally defended Hus's legacy. Although they rejected all
ecclesiastical punishments which could be used by the council to target and
afflict the Hussites, this did not mean that ecclesiastical authority was completely and characteristically rejected. The general mindset was that if a pope
were elected and universally recognized, they would pursue their claims. In
the meantime, the lords were willing to obey their local bishops—provided,
however, that the bishops never commanded anything which was against the
law of God! If the bishops were to command anything against the law of
God, then the university's rector and the doctors of Scripture would be cited
as the final competent authorities. They also unanimously agreed to grant
their priests the freedom to preach the word of God; this clearly exceeded
the boundaries of established canon law (according to which only the bishop
possessed the authority to decide who was eligible to preach). In addition to
the nobility, the university put forward its own official statement. As Bartoš
correctly notes, this was not a mere formal protest by the institution, but a

direct eyewitness account of Hus's colleagues and students. On September 11, 1415, a speech was made which in all likelihood was written by Master Jakoubek of Stříbro. He publicly confessed that Hus was

> an indescribable man—a splendid mirror of holiness, a humble man who prac-
> ticed works of authentic love and incorruptible truth toward everyone, who sur-
> passed everyone with his courageous words and wisdom and became a teacher
> of life to all—a man who has known no equal.[36]

As the university was under the impression that Jerome of Prague (1379–1416) had already perished as well, a heart-touching testimony was brought forward in his honor as well.

A congress of the Bohemian nobility produced a *Protest Petition* (*Stížný list*) against the Church Council in the very same month of its initiation. It was a massive declaration of protest containing seals attached by 452 lords. The document itself was published multiple times.[37] The message was clear: the nobles held the Council of Constance fully responsible and blamed them for condemning unto death Master Jan Hus—a good, righteous, Catholic man whose life, integrity, character, and reputation were without question. According to the lords, Hus had taught the law of God in accordance with church-approved doctors and condemned all heresies and falsehoods. Since he had faithfully led others to embrace love and peace, the diet of lords could not understand that Hus could have fallen into error or could have committed any alleged offense. They further added that Hus had lived a quiet and devout life and had always exhorted others to live in accordance with both the Gospel and the teachings of the church fathers. The diet considered his execution as being conspired and perpetrated under false accusations by enemies of both the Kingdom of Bohemia and the Margraviate of Moravia. The conclusion of the petition protest contained an oath to "promote and defend those who are devout, humble, and consistent in their preaching of the word of our Lord Jesus Christ, discarding all hesitation and willing to shed blood if necessary."[38]

Only one of the original eight copies of the petition survives to this day.[39] Its author is most probably Dr. Jan of Jesenice. More importantly, the very creation of this petition was a form of open revolt and revolution, as their protest makes it clear that the Bohemian nobility will no longer honor canon law and that instead they desire to rule themselves justly and independently. Those who signed the document knew full well that by doing so they would be risking not only their property but also their very lives. In his analysis of the events and the document itself, Bartoš took careful notice of those who had signed the protest petition. From the high Bohemian nobility, there were twenty-seven noble families of thirty-five members represented. The other signatories were mainly comprised of lower nobility. Although the statistics are not important on their own, they do hint at several important elements. For example, if the high nobility had not participated, the protest would have fallen flat. The Church Council responded by placing an interdict on everyone who had signed the document and demanded an official investigation (though it did not actually happen until February of 1416). Unfortunately, it also led to the worsening of conditions for Jerome of Prague, as he remained imprisoned in Constance.

In addition to the interdict, the council also wanted to initiate a case against the archbishop, and even against the king and queen. The Catholic league of the nobility which was activated against the Hussite nobility converted King Václav IV (1361–1419). However, following the return of bishop Jan Železný (d. 1430) from the council, he began to aggressively oppose the laity's receiving the chalice. Although Václav never personally accepted the chalice himself, he desired to maintain peace, so he allowed the Hussites to spread their practices further; and even the queen was supportive of these efforts.

The purpose of the preceding material is not to offer a detailed description of the historical developments of events as they unfolded. Instead, it serves to illustrate that the boundaries of canon law—which were previously imagined to be inviolable—were exceeded, and as a result the entire society changed. If one were to analyze the situation more deeply, it would quickly become obvious that despite all the efforts from the Catholic league, intimidation by force was ultimately ineffective and virtually useless. Contrary to what some might claim, the Catholic Archbishop of Prague Konrád of Vechta (c. 1370–1431) certainly was not a weak or inexperienced player on the Catholic side.[40] Having recognized where the truth lies, he attempted to play the role of mediator rather than to become the voice of the council's demands. Even despite all of his maneuvers (e.g., crowning Sigismund as king against the direct will of the Estates), he ultimately showed his true allegiances in 1421 when he publicly came out in support of the *Four Articles*. As a result, bishop Jan Železný (of Olomouc) and bishop Aleš of Březí (of Litomyšel) denounced his fealty. The pope later deprived him of his office and placed an interdict on his head in 1425; nevertheless, he remained an archbishop for the Hussites and continued to anoint priests for the movement until his death.

From the perspective of Catholic law, Prague experienced a period of *Sede vacante* ("the seat being vacant") which lasted until 1561, at which point the Counter-Reformation movement helped install Catholic Antonín Brus of Mohelnice (1518–1580) as the new Archbishop of Prague. Konrád's successor, Master Jan Rokycana,[41] was elected by the Hussites as the new archbishop, but never acknowledged by the papacy and never received ordination as a bishop. He served as Rector of the University of Prague (1432), and his election to the position of archbishop came from the Bohemian Diet (1435). Rokycana was a living proof of how the state had transformed under the Hussite movement and how confessional and canon law were seen very differently in comparison with previous times.

The council wanted to implement its anti-Hussite decisions in Bohemia at all costs, and the person supposed to implement them was Sigismund of Luxembourg, the brother of Václav IV. Such efforts failed and instead helped preserve the further development of the Hussite movement. Even with the Hussite majority, the struggle of the reform faction at the University of Prague had not been an easy one.[42] Thus far, the gradual transformation of constitutional rights had taken place through unofficial means. While the king remained in place, the real political power had already changed hands and was in favor of the Estates. The final clash with the council, however, was still standing at the doorstep. Pope Martin V, born Otto Colonna (1369–1431), issued a double bull containing all of the council's decrees against the Bohemian Hussites (February 22, 1418), along with a list of conditions under which the Bohemian heretics were expected to surrender.

Before listing the various demands, it must be asserted that above all else this was an effort to enforce the validity of canon law and re-establish the previous state of affairs (i.e., the old order). None of the council members could fathom that such a scenario was no longer possible because a new era was not only on horizon, but was unfolding right before their very eyes. These are the actual stipulations which the council demanded:

> King Václav was to officially swear to restore the validity of the old order, which was to be followed by the same pledge from the Bohemian clergy and the university masters; those who refused to do so were to be punished in accordance with the canon law.
>
> Secular persons who did not appear in court or who defended heretics were also expected to swear to uphold and respect the Council's ruling concerning Wyclif, Hus, and Jerome.
>
> Everything that had been stolen or confiscated from the church was to be returned.
>
> Orthodoxy was to be restored at the University of Prague and its ten prominent masters (Jakoubek, Jesenice, and others) were to be presented for judgment.
>
> All the writings of Wyclif, Hus, and Jakoubek were to be burned.
>
> Preaching without permission of the ecclesiastical authorities was to be prohibited.
>
> All known heretics were to be reported to the Church and whoever was suspected of heresy was to renounce in the most austere manner possible.

All of these stipulations are clear political demands aimed at dissolving the Hussite league. This became especially apparent in the fact that all Hussite priests and laymen convicted of heresy were to be treated as heretics—that is, to be burned at the stake.

One remaining issue, however, related to who would actually enforce these demands. The council eventually separated, and Sigismund was hesitant to wage war against both his half-brother (who had no intention of provoking a civil war) and the kingdom itself (not to mention that his lack of forces to accomplish such a daunting endeavor prevented him from doing so). It was only after his efforts to persuade the various noblemen around Václav utterly failed that the emperor first started threatening the country with a crusade. Yet, the less action he took, the more his speeches became filled with propaganda: how it was necessary to kill heretics and drown their heretical priests.

Essentially, one could say that at the time there was no strong ruling hand in the Crown lands. A major breaking point in the development of the state which managed to influence its legal development was the death of King Václav IV in August of 1419. Before his death, the defenestration of seven town council members appointed by Václav at the New Town Hall in Prague did not necessarily signify any constitutional change, but it certainly demonstrated that the town's inhabitants would also have a major influence in defending the chalice and other Hussite values.

Regarding the issue of royal succession, there was no dispute that Sigismund was supposed to become the next heir of the crown, and herein we find one of the most dangerous moments for the legacy of Jan Hus. The Catholic nobility eagerly looked forward to Sigismund, as they were convinced that the king would not "migrate" to Prague and would leave the government in their hands—in some way repeating the situation which had already happened during the reign of John of Luxembourg (1296–1346),[43] who was Sigismund's grandfather. Even the Hussite nobility was not necessarily against the emperor as their new king, but there was one condition and qualification: the laity's receiving of the chalice had to be endorsed. Though the strength of the Hussite lords was not very great at the beginning, it can be assumed that whatever diplomacy failed to achieve would definitely be accomplished through monetary means. However, a new power was on the rise whose influence would greatly determine (or at least affect) all future developments: the towns and villages with strong Hussite elements.

Bartoš's words are apropos:

In most parts of the country, the conditions of the peasant estate from the great clash of royal power during the lord's revolt were steadily deteriorating and propelled the peasants into a revolution. The nobility, affected by the diminishing purchasing power of money from the peasants' interest tax (i.e., usance), sought to compensate for their losses by abusing the judicial power which they exercised to impose even more taxes and forced labor on their subjects. This uncontrollably cumulative oppression nourished the resistance of the peasantry against the nobility and led to many subjects joining forces with the rebellion. They kindled the revolution by making the greatest of sacrifices—the inexpressible sacrifice of both blood and possessions, with which they "bought back" their victory.[44]

The two factions—the inhabitants of towns and the peasantry—proved to be crucial in the eventually ensuing wars and in further developments. One issue remained problematic from the beginning, and it was only a matter of time before it would have to be resolved. It was clear that Sigismund would actually want to lay hold of his inheritance, and that such an endeavor would be impossible without war. The Hussite side stood against him, being indivisibly unified behind the idea of the chalice. At the outset of the conflict, there was a pressing demand for a more complex and broader program to be formulated. This would prove to be quite difficult, since there were many points of conflict between the various Hussite allies. For example, there were those who understood Hus's legacy in a more radical way than others, wishing to grant communion even to children or refusing to reverence icons. For university masters, this demand was too radical and reflected the differences between Prague and the countryside. One critical point was obvious: if the country were to maintain its resistance against the emperor, then it would be necessary to create a league of Hussite-aligned towns led by Prague (which eventually did come into existence).

The atmosphere in society was excited and energized. In addition to Prague, many religious pilgrimages were being celebrated, of which the most widely known was the pilgrimage to *na Křížkách* on September 30, 1419. It resulted in various acts of violence which necessitated intervention. The societal atmosphere of that turbulent autumn has been described in great detail by Kaminsky,[45] who was well aware of the religious significance of these events and also realized their impact for both the law and the organization of society itself.

The Prague Diet adopted for the first time the foundation of the Hussite program which would later become the renowned *Four Articles of Prague*; those articles were built upon the legacy of Master Jan Hus and also signified the expansion and clarification of his ideals.

NOTES

1. For a helpful comparative look at the age preceding Hus, see František Michálek Bartoš, *Čechy v době Husově 1378–1415* (Prague: Jan Laichter, 1947). Some of Bartoš's conclusions have since been disproven by new research, but his overall description of that period remains valid.

2. See note 7.

3. Kejř, "Jan Hus jako právní myslitel," 197.

4. These works are found in *Corpus Iuris Canonici*, vol. 2, ed. Emil Friedberg (Leipzig: Bernhard Tauchnitz, 1881).

5. Hus mistakenly attributed this work to Boniface VIII due to the common practice of copying from contemporary manuscripts.

6. The *Glossa Ordinaria* is published as volumes 113 and 114 of the *Patrologia Latina (PL)*. However, in the Migne (PL) edition, in addition to misattributing the Gloss to Strabo, there are several omissions, including the biblical prologues and the complete Vulgate text.

7. Kejř, "Jan Hus jako právní myslitel," 197.

8. See František Ryšánek, et al., eds., *Magistri Iohannis Hus Opera Omnia*, 25 vols. (Prague: Academia, 1959–), 22:19–37. Henceforth *Magistri Iohannis Hus Opera Omnia*.

9. *M. Jana Husi Korespondence a dokumenty*, ed. Václav Novotný (Praha: Nákladem komise pro vydávání pramenů náboženského hnutí českého, 1920), 19–26.

10. See *Magistri Iohannis Hus Opera Omnia*, 1:285–293.

11. Kejř, "Jan Hus jako právní myslitel," 198.

12. Ibid.

13. Ibid., 199.

14. Ibid. Cf. Kejř, *Husův proces*. In this important work, Kejř formulated the thesis that Hus was the instrument of his own demise, since he did not realize that he was not attending a disputation but rather a court trial and thus should have reacted accordingly.

15. (Translator's note: This Czech verb also connotes managing, governing, and leading.)

16. *Magistri Iohannis Hus Opera Omnia*, 19A:17–22, 169–175.

17. *Magistri Iohannis Hus Opera Omnia*, 24:39–79.

18. For Wyclif's influence, see Amedeo Molnár and František Mrázek Dobiáš, eds., *Husova výzbroj do Kostnice; Řeč o míru, O postačitelnosti Kristova zákona, Řeč o víře, Prohlášení o článcích Pálčových* (Prague: Ústřední církevní nakladatelství, 1965), 168–172.

19. Kejř, "Jan Hus jako právní myslitel," 200.

20. Ibid. Kejř first used this term in a lecture during a Prague symposium concerning the relationship of the Bohemian Reformation to the Reformation of the sixteenth century.

21. Bohumil Ryba, ed., *Magistri Iohannis Hus Quodlibet* (Prague: Orbis, 1948), 125, 171–172.

22. Kejř, "Jan Hus jako právní myslitel," 200.

23. Václav Flajšhans, ed., *Spisy M. Jana Husi*, vol. 6, *Super IV Sententiarum*, part 3 (Prague: Vilímek, 1906), 3:723: "*De iusticia autem, que materialiter sic diffinitur, quod est tribuere unicuique, quod suum est, planum est, quod Deo anthonomastice convenit, cum solum ipse potest debitum singulis tam largiter inpertiri; et cum in eo non sit habitus distinctus a sua essencia, patet, quod essencia divina sit virtus iusticie et per consequens prima iusticia. Et patet, que iusticia et quomodo conpetit ipsi Deo.*"

24. Ibid., 201.

25. Husi, *Super IV Sententiarum*, 3:644–694.

26. *M. Jana Husi Korespondence a dokumenty*, ed. Václav Novotný (Praha: Nákladem komise pro vydávání pramenů náboženského hnutí českého, 1920), 133: "*hanc appellacionem offero Ihesu Christo, iudici iustissimo, qui noscit, protegit et iudicat, manifestat et premiat indefectibiliter cuiuslibet hominis iustam causam.*"

27. Kejř, "Jan Hus jako právní myslitel," 202.

28. Vlastimil Kybal, *M. Jan Hus: život a učení*, 3 vols. (Prague: Jan Laichter, 1923–1931).

29. Paul de Vooght, *L'hérésie de Jean Huss*, 2nd ed. (Louvain: Bureaux de la Revue Bibliothèque de l'Université, 1975). A Czech translation by Libuše Havlíčková was published in several editions of *Theologická Revue* by the Hussite Theological Faculty between 1997 and 2002. There are plans for an English translation of Vooght's classic French work by Jacob Marques Rollison and Angelo Franklin.

30. Kejř, "Jan Hus jako právní myslitel," 203.

31. See Paul de Vooght, *Jacobellus de Stribro (†1429). Premier théologien du hussitisme* (Louvain: Publications universitaires de Louvain, 1972, 351–386.

32. Jakoubek of Stříbro, *Qui non diligit me*, f. 221v: "*lex Christi, eius vita, doctrina et vita suorum apostolorum debent esse nobis primum metrum et mensura omnium agendorum.*"

33. Jan Rokycana mentioned this in his sermon entitled "V úterý velikonoční." See Jan Rokycana, *Postilla*, ed. František Šimek, 2 vols. (Prague: České Akademii Věd a Umění, 1928–1929), 693.

34. On June 21, 1415, Hus wrote a letter to Master Havlík, the preacher in Bethlehem Chapel, in which he expressed his conviction concerning the sacrament. "Do not oppose the sacrament of the Lord's cup which the Lord instituted through himself and through his apostle. For no Scripture is opposed to it, but only a custom which I imagine has sprung up by negligence. We should not follow custom but the example of Christ and truth. . . . Also, dearly beloved, prepare yourself for suffering on account of partaking of the bread and the communion of the cup. . . . You will find the reasons for the communion of the cup in what I have written in Constance." Novotný, *Korespondence*, 294–295.

35. Hus also mentions this in the same letter to Master Havlík on June 21, 1415. The official declaration of the council is found in *Decrees of the Ecumenical Councils*, ed. Norman P. Tanner (Washington, DC: Georgetown University Press, 1990) 1:418–419.

36. Bartoš, *Husitská revoluce*, 1:16.

37. See Václav Novotný, *Hus v Kostnici a česká šlechta: poznámky a dokumenty* (Prague: Nákladem Společnosti přátel starožitností českých v Praze, 1915).

38. Ibid., 76.

39. See Edinburgh University Library MS P.C. 73.

40. For the most recent work on Konrád, see the entry in Milan Buben, *Encyklopedie českých a moravských sídelních biskupů* (Prague: Logik, 2000), 363–368.

41. For the classic work concerning his life and teachings, see František Šimek, *Učení M. Jana Rokycany* (Prague: Nákladem České akademie věd a umění, 1938); see also *Život a dílo Mistra Jana z Rokycan: svědectví Zdeňka Nejedlého, Kamila Krofty, Martina Kozáka a Josefa Teigeho*, ed. Petros Cironis (Rokycany: Státní okresní archiv, 1997); see also Petros Cironis, *Život a dílo Mistra Jana z Rokycan* (Rokycany: Státní okresní archiv Rokycany, 1997).

42. Ivana Čornejová et al., *Dějiny Univerzity Karlovy*, vol. 1 (Prague: Univerzita Karlova, 1995), 27–100, 135–162. This struggle has already been explained in sufficient detail. See Václav Vladivoj Tomek, *Děje university pražské* (Prague: W kommissí u Řiwnáče, 1849); see also Palacký, *Dějiny národu českého*, 3:335–417; see also *Dějiny Univerzity Karlovy*, vols. 1–4 (Prague: Karolinum, 2009).

43. He is also known as John of Bohemia and John the Blind.

44. Bartoš, *Husitská revoluce*, 1:68.

45. Kaminsky, *A History of the Hussite Revolution*, 265–309.

Chapter 2

The *Four Articles of Prague*
A Political and Legal Program

Karel Malý is correct in his claims that the legal sources from the Hussite period that are of central importance are relatively scant.[1] Those sources that are available usually take the form of a religious or political manifesto, and they reveal much information about the form of law and legal consciousness. They first reverberated during the congress of towns led by Prague in 1419, where they were adopted by all Hussite parties present and were subsequently brought together into a precise form in the face of foreign intervention during May 1420.

According to Bartoš, their author was Master Jakoubek of Stříbro, who himself indirectly acknowledged as much. Jakoubek "was instrumental at that moment in giving a truly exquisite expression to the desires of the burgeoning revolution. We can then find them in all of their peremptory expressions, in records of town diets and congresses as well as in manifestos which testify against both domestic and foreign opponents. Furthermore, they were the basis of the peace treaty which the revolution finally achieved after seventeen years of fighting."[2]

Malý stated that this program was a

> fundamental legal norm invoked by the groups within the Hussite movement, though naturally its contents were interpreted according to suit their needs and the demands at hand. The *Articles* as a lapidary expression of the movement's program and aims became an integral part of all the essential documents of the Hussite movement, and ultimately became the foundation for the Compacts of Basel—the peace treaty between the Church Council and the Hussites which was ratified in Jihlava on July 5, 1436—which later became part of the Bohemian constitution. Swearing to uphold its principles was mandatory for all kings of Bohemia up until the Battle of White Mountain.[3]

The "side-by-side" characteristics of the *Four Articles* as presented by a historian and a lawyer clearly demonstrate their importance. There is a vast wealth of literature detailing with this topic, especially from a historical perspective. In the following pages, proper attention will be focused on their legal relevance, with the studies by Malý and his teacher Vaněček serving as primary guides. In analyzing the *Four Articles* as a political and legal program of the Hussite movement, one must bear several important facts in mind: the arguments utilized within are based upon Scripture, the lives of saints, and the fathers and teachers of the church. Given the expertise of their argumentation, it is clear that they originated from the University of Prague; nonetheless, the argumentation "conscientiously diverges from the official teachings of the Church; and entirely in the spirit of Hus's appearance in Constance, Church dogma was being measured by one's own interpretation of the Bible, which according to Hus was the decisive argument in his conflict with both the Church and the Council."[4] At the same time, the rationale is not dogmatic but rests upon a rational interpretation (i.e., it is possible to interpret the Bible according to reason). Precedence was primarily given to the New Testament, which was seen as the truth of Christ—the evangelical truth (*lex Christi*). "*Lex Dei* becomes the basic criteria by which one can judge not only the actions of individuals and even the Church itself, but it simultaneously serves as a framework for deciding whether or not to obey the orders of unworthy lord, sovereign, or authority."[5]

The *Four Articles* have been preserved in various forms. As Malý points out, one such edition (which was included in the chiliastic writings of Tábor) was formulated in a much stricter manner and reveals how the *Four Articles* were used in the local radical community. The list of demands included "liberating every truth, spreading the praise of God, pursuing mankind's salvation, and destroying sins."[6] Similarities with at least two of the articles are quite obvious. Malý asserts that the argumentation presented in the articles, which was based on biblical texts and church authorities, was intended to facilitate an easy adoption of their program. One of the reasons why the *Four Articles* were even brought forward at all, inter alia, was the fact that they were intended to be included among the requirements for Sigismund, who was to become the king of Bohemia. While that is doubtlessly true, one must remember that a different line of reasoning (i.e., argumentations of a secular character) was not even possible in the first place. If the articles were to appeal only to reason or logical thinking, no one at the time would have taken them seriously at all.

In terms of a just and new legal order, one of the articles (usually counted as the fourth) was especially important, as it called for punishing mortal sins (crimes) that were contrary to the law of God—regardless of the perpetrator's social status. On the one hand, this would obstruct (perhaps even abolish) the ecclesiastical jurisdiction over its members, since according to this demand it would enable even those of the clergy to be held accountable and punished by secular powers; on the other hand, it marks the first instance of civil equality being declared before the law. Malý draws attention to the surrounding historical context: relations between the Bohemian Estates and the monarch shifted considerably in the spring of 1420. Sigismund was deprived of the throne at the Hussite Diet on the 18th of April, and though he later besieged Prague, the crusaders which he commanded during the Battle of the Vítkov Hill in July of the same year were subsequently defeated.

Legal questions once again rose to the forefront of everyone's mind, primarily those centered around loyalty demanded to the king and the possibilities of resistance against an unworthy ruler *(ius resistendi et ius contradicendi)*. Malý points out that the Bohemian constitution had no such option at the time, although there were similar provisions in other countries (e.g., *The Golden Bull of 1222* in Hungary or the English *Magna Charta* from 1215). The Bohemian Estates, on the other hand, had no legal basis or rights which would enable them to dethrone a ruling monarch in accordance with the law of God, so it was necessary for them to formulate it themselves. Malý notes that the inspiration came from Wyclif's works regarding disloyal or unfaithful stewardship as presented by Jakoubek of Stříbro.[7] Other arguments made by Jakoubek from the same year (1420) are provocative; he explained that the people have the right both to participate in war even without a king, as well as to depose an unworthy or malevolent king. This is essentially a proclamation of the right to revolution and rebellion. However, when the proclamation is placed in its historical context, the conclusion emerges as obvious: Sigismund rejected the law of God by denying the chalice to the laymen, and thus lost any right to the throne.

According to Malý, this demand was truly revolutionary and is based on the fourth article, which states that it is possible to punish any ruler who compromised the law of God. This was justified by the fact that the law of God applies to all equally, regardless of one's social standing, rank, position, or status. The primary purpose of such a stipulation was to prevent the abuse of the canon law and of the special jurisdiction enjoyed by members of the clergy, since under normal circumstances only an archbishop (i.e., the ecclesiastical authority) was eligible to punish those within the ecclesiastical hierarchy. The requirement of equality for all secular individuals before the law of God was something *nouveau*, since even the monarch himself was subject to this court.

One of the oldest surviving versions of the *Four Articles* does not feature biblical quotations, but merely a reference to the apostle Paul and his claims that those who should be punished for transgressions are not only the sinners themselves but also those who enable or allow sinfulness in the first place—and in these cases, they "deserve to die." That is not to say that the articles lacked biblical proofs for their argumentation, since they are present in other parts of the text itself. However, references to later legal standards are almost entirely absent. The few that remain apply the principle which was later formulated in the so-called Judge of Cheb (1432), which declared that Scripture should be the judge between the Hussites and the Catholics. Although it allows for the church's traditions (i.e., all legal documents and rulings), it does so only when they are in accordance with Scripture. Although the Judge of Cheb itself (*iudex in Egra compactatus*) was a treaty with eleven main points (i.e., articles) and came into being later, it arose from and agreed with Hussite practice. Therefore, it directly followed Hus and the *Four Articles* and forms an integral part of the Hussite legal and argumentative tradition.

If one were to read the fourth article superficially, it might seem that it is merely a collection of demands concerning the application of secular laws for all equally. After all, the article states that actions such as "'fornication, gluttony, theft, murder, deceit, fraud, bearing false witness, witchcraft, dishonest business, possessing illegally gained goods, and usury' are criminal offenses."[8]

It is also true that the fourth article primarily focuses on transgressions committed by clergymen and that such offenses are deemed as acts which oppose God himself; this perfectly corresponds with a medieval concept of criminal law. Karel Malý precisely describes in which way this requirement of the fourth article was new: it is the demand for the abrogation of legal differences of offenders according to status or rank before the court. Notice the precise and exact qualification: "It was a proclamation of requirements that differ significantly from the existing concept of medieval law and justice. The emphatic enforcing of social inequality in administering the regulations of criminal law (which was rather typical for fourteenth-century Bohemia) was giving way to a new set of ideas. According to the fourth article, the principle of private initiative was to be abandoned and replaced by the official interest of the country's good reputation (i.e., to clear the country from its bad and false reputation). Furthermore, the differences between the social positions (i.e., ranks), including the concessions and privileges which they have so far enjoyed in the area of criminal law, disappear. The demand for equality in court is beginning to loom large, at least in terms of criminal liability for the crime committed. This fully corresponds to the model of evangelism echoing from Tábor, and relates to Jan Hus's conception regarding a mutual social contract between lords (including the monarch) and their subjects."[9] This legal historian is also correct in recognizing that the demand for equality in the Hussite movement is based on Scripture—the same as in many other reform movements—and in one form or another was inspired by the poverty of Jesus Christ and the early church. From a legal standpoint, it would be enlightening to research and trace the arguments employed within these various movements.[10]

The main position detailed in Hussite argumentations is that anyone entrusted with power is accountable to God. On the other hand, while their subjects tend to obey only that which is beneficial to them, it is nonetheless still within their right to refuse obedience toward unworthy authorities or the king. Here one can see Wyclif's influence upon Hus and his teachings, as evidenced in his speech in Constance: "For whoever is in mortal sin is not a worthy king before God."[11] There is a constant appeal that even lords are subject to the law of God, which would necessitate that secular law must be in conformity with the divine law as well. Ecclesiastical law, naturally, was not mentioned, since by its very nature it must correspond to the law of God— that is, to Scripture—or it is invalid. Before leaving this short analysis of the fourth article, reference will be made Malý's explanation of the punishment appropriate for those violating the law of God.

The punishment of criminals and offenders of God's law was a complex affair among the Hussites, as there was no united agreement or consensus on the issue. Especially problematic were the doubts which they entertained concerning capital punishment. In particular, this is not because the Hussites necessarily viewed life as sacred in and of itself, but because it would take away from the executed sinner the opportunity to repent and make restitution for his sins and to obtain God's forgiveness and salvation. In fact, many Hussite synods were concerned with solving this theological question.

Of course, views on the death penalty were radical in Tábor, both for the chiliastic group and for Žižka himself. Žižka especially was renowned for killing his enemies not only on the field of battle but also for pouring red-hot molten lead down the throats of captured prisoners who refused to accept the chalice during the Eucharist. The masters of Prague were reluctant to receive the chalice and distanced themselves from these actions. For example, Master Jakoubek criticized any lord who was quick to punish sins yet did not at the same time live according to the law of God himself. That is not to say that he denied their authority over the people, as he along with Master Christian of Prachatice

acknowledged the right of lords to exercise criminal jurisdiction over their subjects in defense of the law of God. The criteria therefore became the law of God itself, which in its application rendered legal norms invalid if they were in contradiction to it (i.e., it excluded the validity of conflicting legal norms). Jakoubek of Stříbro adhered to such views even prior to the Hussite Revolution, and it is no coincidence that some of his earlier reflections can be seen as a foreshadowing of the formulation of the fourth article.[12]

We now turn to the actual wording of the articles, as it is an important and yet difficult topic to cover. This difficulty stems primarily from the fact that multiple versions of the text exist which are cited inconsistently across various sources. There is also the further problem of independent readings, since the various groups perceived the texts according to their own ideological positions. For example, *Staré letopisy české (Old Bohemian Annals)* by František Palacký presented an account that is distinctly different from the account offered by Vavřinec of Březová (c. 1370–1437)[13]; a complete analysis of this issue would require a lengthy monograph of its own. The version chosen for this work is considered to be the authoritative text.[14] Its origins can be traced to "several old (vague) manuscripts" issued by František Palacký.[15] The editors made only minimal corrections which were duly noted in the preface.[16] According to them, the version in question originated from early July in 1420. They also made reference to all of the important secondary literary sources of the time (up until 1951) which focused on the *Four Articles*. This edition will be used to introduce the particular wording of the articles along with additional comments concerning various readings which are considered important from the perspective of the law.

The preamble of the *Four Articles* should be sufficient to help one discern the historical context related to their origin:

> To everyone in general and especially to every Christian, let it be solemnly known and announced that the Bohemian community and faithful Christians stand in divine hope, and with God's help—as far as they are possibly able with all of their possessions[17] and with their own life, even unto death—intend to stand against all of those who are in opposition to this: establishing and legislating[18] nothing else other than these four Christian articles commanded by our Lord Jesus Christ in the New Testament.[19]

The German text, addressed to those who had besieged Prague in July, provides information concerning the cause of the war with Sigismund and his allies. In the preamble to the German text the blame for current events is not laid upon Sigismund's shoulders as one might expect, but is instead laid on the church itself, and particularly on the king's priests and his allies who "seduced the clergymen to oppress the faithful."[20] The kingdom did not want to accept Sigismund as king because he did not accept the articles; those in the kingdom who were faithful to God would have otherwise accepted him. "He might have consented, but some bishops and greedy priests were said to have led him astray."[21]

The presented position was obvious, yet clearly open to further negotiations at the same time. Sigismund lost neither his candidacy for the throne nor was he *a priori* excluded. In a way, this position anticipated the approach adopted many years later—although that would only take place after an enormous amount of blood had been shed and many lives were lost. At the time when the articles were presented, however, no one could predict in advance the exact way in which the struggle for loyalty to the law of God would eventually end.

The first article reads as follows: "*First:* The word of God should be proclaimed and preached throughout the Kingdom of Bohemia freely and without any hindrance from Christian priests, just as our Savior commands." The article then references its biblical source material, including Matt. 28:19 and Mark 16:15, as well as some passages from the apostle Paul. Since the references mentioned are more or less general, a greater interest should be concerned with ascertaining where exactly the legal binding power of this article and its originality existed. Even at first glance, the main concern clearly appears to be freedom of speech, though of course there was also substantially more at stake. According to the canon law of the church, only those who had been properly ordained and who were within the proper ecclesiastical jurisdiction and were commissioned by their bishop or a higher ecclesiastical authority (e.g., the pope) could preach the word of God. In this way, the church was able control all of those whom it allowed to serve as preachers while also maintaining a firm grip on the content of the message that was actually being preached. At the same time, becoming an ordained priest in medieval times was not as difficult to achieve as some might imagine. It was certainly no exception to find bishops who were willing to buy positions in exchange for money. Yet, the ordination of priests itself was insufficient on its own to make one eligible for the priestly vocation. As a rule, those who were ordained fell under the jurisdiction of the one who had consecrated them; however, if he ever left to go somewhere else or came into conflict with the one who ordained him, his permission was revoked, and he could no longer give sermons or sacraments to the public. Administering the sacraments was tied to prebends, but what happened when the ordained person did not have a prebend? The pre-Hussite period witnessed a large number of so-called *vacant clerics*—clerics who were paid to represent someone else, who (although properly ordained and installed) found other tasks to be much more lucrative. Many of Hus's predecessors also criticized this unholy dissension. In addition to the "the freedom of speech," the first article was also aiming at the dissolution of the existing practices of canon law and church practice. The article assumes that if someone is properly ordained to serve, then he is commissioned by Christ himself to perform his priestly duties and freely preach the word of God.

Later there was a conflict regarding the insertion in the first Prague article which stipulated that only those ordained for preaching the word of God should be given freedom to do so. Even so, this could be interpreted in a twofold manner: if it were construed to mean "those who were ordained" (i.e., by receiving ordination), then it would pose no problem; however, there was an attempt to interpret this parenthetical expression in the sense of the ordination of the ecclesiastical authorities acting in accord with the secular authorities.

With its demand for freedom from the requirements of canon law, the first article was certainly revolutionary. It would not be a daring exaggeration to consider it as a demand for secularization, since it meant liberating the gospel from the existing legal and power structures. Many prominent thinkers in the later period of the Bohemian Reformation also understood this demand in the same vein, and it was also similarly appraised by the reform movements within Czech Catholicism in the not-so-distant past.[22]

Even the second article does not seem overtly theological at first glance; yet once again this assumption is not completely accurate. It is written thus: "*Second:* The blessed sacrament of the body and blood of Christ should be given freely under both kinds to all faithful Christians who are not burdened with mortal sin, according to the institution and commandment of our Lord and Savior." This is followed by biblical evidence and supporting materials from church tradition, mainly from church fathers such as Gregory the Great, Augustine of Hippo, Jerome of Stridonium, Cyprian of Carthage, Ambrose of Milan, and others. As already established above, the Hussites had nothing against making use of church tradition (which includes not only the works of church fathers but also the decisions reached by various church councils and synods) as long as they were not contrary to Scripture. In the case of communion under both kinds (*sub utraque specie*), the result was clear: not only was it completely in line with biblical teachings but the practices of the church in antiquity in both the West and the East proved its validity. The fact that it was also served during the Middle Ages was without question. This practice persisted in the East, which is one of the reasons why the Hussites were in contact with the Orthodox Church before the fall of Constantinople in 1453.[23] In the West it gradually disappeared at the turn of the millennium, until the practice of communion under one kind was officially decreed at the Fourth Lateran Council in 1215. It was certainly a theological question, and a vast amount of research has been dedicated to it. It is also a question which the Roman Catholic Church would have been willing to discuss if the whole issue were not inextricably linked to the context of its conflict with Jan Hus. The Council of Constance (1414–1418) officially condemned the practice of the laity receiving from the chalice on June 15, 1415, and considered the matter settled.[24] This is why the council was incensed when word reached its ears that the chalice for the laity had spread in Prague, considering it an act of rebellion against the church's authority and undoubtedly connected with the cause of Jan Hus.

By the time its answer reached Bohemia during the summer of 1417, it was rather obvious that the Hussites would never abandon the chalice and their demand for receiving it. In response, the council debated the issue again on August 20, 1417. It was here that one of the most important figures—Jean Gerson (1363–1429), Chancellor of the University of Paris—reached a principled position and proposed a response which was soon adopted by the rest of the council. Essentially, Gerson rejected any further negotiations and suggested that the easiest solution would be to use military intervention and put any further resistance to the sword.[25] The Bohemians' struggle for the chalice is captivating in many ways—not only before the *Four Articles* appeared but also during the subsequent times of the Basel Compacts, and then to the very end of the Bohemian Reformation. One of its key elements is that the demands of the Bohemian side were supported by the overwhelming majority of the Bohemian nobility, which led to gradual changes in the constitutional conditions. The issue of the chalice being received by the laity also distinguished the kingdom from the Empire, as well as the rest of the *Roman curia.* It is not difficult to agree with Václav Vaněček in his assertion that

> the nobility was primarily concerned with ensuring the sovereignty (as we would call it today) of the Bohemian state against the Roman Empire and the papacy, and with advancing a few of their own professional interests common to both lords and knights. In addition, the Prague towns later added their own conditions.[26]

From a general point of view, the requirement of the laity being able to receive the chalice was a specific kind of equality of the clergy and secular people, since they were both to receive in the same manner—under both kinds. This would mean the end of the clergy's privileged position as a specially chosen social class guaranteed by the established religious order. The lay chalice eventually led to further religious reform: the specific rejection of several liturgical regulations, ceremonies, extravagant pomp, and the use of statues and images. As Vaněček explains, the demands of the first article (preaching the word of God freely) contributed to the increasing call for church services to be performed in the native language.[27] Thus, one can undoubtedly mark the lay chalice and the late medieval efforts for receiving communion under both kinds for all people in Bohemia as a struggle for equality in a time where concepts of equality were not yet quite attainable.

In comparison with the second article, the third proved to be much more revolutionary, as it noticeably interfered with the feudal *status quo* of the time.

> *Third:* Since many priests and monks are exercising rights of civil dominion over a great amount of material goods—violating the commandment of Christ, hindering their priestly office, and causing great detriment to the lords of the

secular estate—unlawful dominion should be taken away and deprived from such priests in order that they can live according to the gospel and be brought back to the way of life of Christ and the apostles.

Once again, the evidence provided had originated from Scripture rather than tradition, while those few elements which were drawn from tradition were of a more general character. Given the plethora of historical sources detailing the opulent lifestyle prevalent in the church and the wealth it amassed while enjoying its secular reign, there is no need to justify the fact that this "secular reign" was one of the main reasons why nearly everyone in society agreed that the church as an institution should be resolutely opposed. A similar phenomenon can be observed more than a century later in Germany on the threshold of the German Reformation. While the Church was preaching noble ideals, in reality, it was acting as a secular institution that desired more and more secular power and influence. It is not as if the secular powers were blameless in the whole affair, due to the fact that they often supported the uncontrolled growth of church power in every way possible. The reign of Charles IV is a typical example of this: the monarch always supported the church in all of its endeavors. When the Bohemian nobility first united against the church (i.e., in their petition protesting the execution of Jan Hus), it was inevitable that property rights and wealth would play a role in the coming conflict. The church rose up against the nobility, and the ecclesiastical domains were immediately occupied. The nobility as well as the towns were enriched, which added an entirely new element.

In towns, not only was church property tampered with, but also (and even predominantly so) the property of the German patriciate. Led by the council of the Old Town of Prague, the new and revolutionary town councils issued decrees ordering the confiscation of all property belonging to those who did not join the movement, especially those who fled the town during such turbulent times. This property was sold off to the burghers for cheap prices afterwards. At the same time all priests who refused to serve communion under both kinds were stripped of their position, and Hussite priests were appointed in their place.[28]

All of this had already occurred as early as 1417 and only intensified as time went on, as it became clear that the conflict would culminate sooner or later. It was the death of Václav in August 1419 that had served as a catalyst for the further acceleration of events. In towns, the general communities (plenary meetings) of all burghers were of decisive importance; they were a type of ruling body correctly described as "democratic, radical, and revolutionary bodies. Whereas before they had only existed on paper, now they became a full-functioning entity."[29] Here the very radical and revolutionary process can be seen in action: it was an attempt to liquidate the ecclesiastical landlords of landed estates (analogous to secular feudal lords). As far as constitutional measures are concerned, the *Four Articles* appeared in the legal order of the Bohemian state in 1421, when the articles became one of the fundamental principles. Never again would the church have a position of dominant power in the land as it had maintained before, since a thorough secularization of its property occurred. The year 1620 saw a certain return of influential church status to a limited degree, but that "recovery" occurred under a completely different set of circumstances—without even mentioning its enforcement by a foreign power.

The influence of the fourth article has already been explained above. Its importance for the history of law lies primarily in its emphasis on the equality of all people before the secular law. It is worded as follows:

Fourth: All mortal sins and especially those sins committed publicly as well as other contemptible offenses against the law of God should be properly and reasonably prohibited and prevented in each estate by those who possess the authority to do so, in order that the ignoble reputation afflicting the Kingdom of Bohemia and its language would be cleansed and its good name restored. Furthermore, as Saint Paul declares, it is not merely the one who commits these sins who is deserving of death, but also those who consent and enable others to commit them (Rom 1:32). Among the common people there exist the sins of fornication, gluttony, theft, murders, lies, deceit, perjury, witchcraft, fraudulent and destructive crafts and commerce, avarice, usury, and other evils similar to these; but among the clergy there exists the heresy of simony by extorting money from baptism, from confirmation, from confessions, from the sacraments of holy communion and anointing with holy oil, from weddings, and charging fees for serving thirty masses and other requiems, vigils, or other prayers purchased or reserved in advance on interest, for funerals, for singing or ringing bells in church, from the consecration of new priests, chapels, altars, cemeteries, for indulgences, for bishoprics and archbishoprics, provosts, the diaconates, parishes, for every chaplaincy, for exchanges, for bulls and also other letters, and for all kinds of benefices and dignities and other spiritual things bought for any price at all, and other innumerable evils and heresies which derive from these are a heretical blight which defiles the holy Church. There are also other iniquities and sins such as pride, greed, adultery, concubinage and other impurities, wrath, envy, quarreling and dissensions, contentions, and indignant citations and frivolous lawsuits, personal payments, offertories, as well as money and other property gained for churches and buildings through hypocritical begging and by making false promises using pretentious words to the simple-minded who are thereby extorted and victimized. Every faithful Christian is duty-bound to hate all of these are sins even as he is [obliged] to hate the father of them (who is the devil himself), and he should oppose, reprimand, and prevent them in accordance to his calling.

Aside from the obvious fact that the fourth article intended equality of all people before the law, it also listed enough criminal offenses to create an entirely new codex. Secular crimes are rather obvious in nature, but it is the spiritual wrongdoings (i.e., criminal acts) of the clergy themselves that are of main importance here. This is primarily because they are essentially crimes from the point of view of morality rather than from the view of canon law. After all, it was possible (i.e., legal) to pay for ceremonies, to buy offices, or bribe someone to create a document or certificate. It is only the moral demands stemming from Hus's legacy which criminalized such grotesque behavior.

Karel Malý tried to analyze how the postulates mentioned in the fourth article were applied within the Hussite movement. The most prominent example would be the so-called *Military Order of Žižka* from April 7, 1423, which is actually a legal source of an official nature.[30] The preamble clearly states that following the *Four Articles* is an essential duty of all of the members of the Brotherhood. As Malý realized, the wording of the last article in Prague was substantially adjusted toward total legal equality: "For we have to halt, disrupt and always stand against sin, both mortal and otherwise, within ourselves first and foremost; then within kings, princes and lords, within the burghers, craftsmen and serfs—in people of both genders and all generations without exception, whether they be young or old."[31] Here one can see the uniform legal responsibility for all people, with the text going so far as to mention the equality of genders before the law. The same author then searches for specific traces of the fourth article within Žižka's *Military Order*. Some of the examples he lists include: the punishment for breaching of discipline during troop movements; guard duty; violating the rules regarding the distribution of spoils, causing internal fighting; wounding, maiming, or killing; and the death penalty for desertion. It is absolutely certain that the *Four Articles* were considered as an essential and fundamental legal norm with which other rules had to comply.

What Malý correctly realized, however, is that the demand for equality of responsibility within society

did not mean social freedom or freedom for the various subjects of lords, since it did not revoke their dependency, nor did it affect the structures of professional power that affected the medieval social classes. What the Hussite theorists (especially the masters of Prague) were establishing was equal legal responsibility for all citizens, and this had its roots in the generally assumed and universally shared responsibility of mankind to observe the law of God. However, this obligation was not hindered by the social hierarchy and professional structure of society. This concept of equality therefore consisted only in the fact that the offender's social status did not exclude liability for the crime. Punishment should be the same for all. The only equality the concept sought to create was one before the court where the sentence was the same for everyone, regardless of their background.[32]

In this explanation, Malý corrects some of the earlier Marxist interpretations without denying the revolutionary character of the *Four Articles of Prague* in any significant way. He sees the primary novelty of the articles in their allowing disobedience to an unworthy lord who contradicts the law of God. He notes that there is an attempt

> to transform dogmatic principles based on the Bible into a practical legal form of life: in cases where legal norms were missing, faith and theology were commonly accepted as valid legal principles in the process of revolution. Legal consciousness became synonymous with them and legal practice accepted them. This is, after all, the model which we find even in other later revolutionary events. Instead of Christian ideology, however, philosophy and the ideology of the revolutionary echelon and social groups succeeds. In this regard, the unmistakable identity of the Hussite example is connected with later developments.[33]

It comes as no surprise that the "legal-theological" ideas first expressed by Hus in a rudimentary form find their full development in the *Four Articles*, transcending the boundaries of both canon law and secular laws of the time and becoming firmly entrenched in the beginning European Reformation. Nevertheless, similar themes are shared by both streams of the "Reformation" which present opportunities for an appropriate, comparative study.[34] An example of this is the important role played by the secular aristocracy on the secularization of property as well as on the administration of ecclesial affairs (confessional law).

In addition to the actual text of the *Four Articles* which was introduced and commented on above, its epilogue also deserves special mention. The authors implore those who seek to implement the articles not to trust anyone who speaks against the articles and instead to view them as a false witness. They proclaim before God that their desire is to do nothing more than to carry out his will, since it must be done and that they simply cannot do otherwise:

> Should any person seem to suffer harm by us, it would be due to dire necessity, since we must defend the law of God and ourselves against the violence and cruelty of God's enemies and our own. And above all, we confess that if we give another any reason to suspect us of evil, we are ready and willing to improve our ways and wholeheartedly accept the teachings of the Holy Scripture.[35]

It is important to mention once again the community of Tábor which began to organize itself in the spring of 1420. Both of the unique monographs by Macek[36] and by Šmahel[37] provide all of the necessary research, as the role played by the community is intriguing from a legal perspective but ultimately not crucial in the grand scheme of things.

In the disputation regarding the Judge of Cheb as well as the *Compactata* themselves, Tábor was present through a representative, yet they did not have a decisive role in the ongoing negotiations. Their influence and role had gradually been declining since 1434, yet this does not change the fact that during the first months of their existence, they started their new life completely independent of the framework of the feudal system and the existing Bohemian state. The structure of the community was truly revolutionary at the time since it was led by four elected elders. The Tábor Union later became divided into three main groups: the peasants, the military power, and the domestic communities, which organized themselves according to Tábor's example and yet remained distinct from one another. The field troops were each led by their own hetman and elders, whereas the nonmilitary head of the Tábor communities was a governor (also called a ruler). The influence exercised by the Tábor Union was due to its many allies among the other towns such as Písek, Prachatice, Sušice, Horažďovice, Klatovy, and Domažlice. However, Tábor had very little impact on further legal and constitutional developments. Having now explored the four articles themselves, we will now endeavor to trace the contours of the struggle for the character of the Hussite Bohemian state in subsequent years based on available historical sources and literature.

NOTES

1. Malý, "K právnímu odkazu husitství," 208.
2. Bartoš, *Husitská revoluce*, 1:71.
3. Malý, "K právnímu odkazu husitství," 208.
4. Ibid., 209.
5. Ibid.
6. Jan z Příbramě, "Život kněží Táborských," in *Ktož jsú boží bojovníci: čtení o Taboře v husitském revolučním hnutí*, ed. Josef Macek (Praha: Melantrich, 1951), 269–270. A new edition is found in *Jan z Příbramě: Život kněží Táborských*, ed. Jaroslav Boubín (Podbrdsko, Fontes 1) (Příbram: Státní okresní archiv Příbram: Okresní muzeum Příbram, 2000).
7. For Jakoubek's Czech translation of Wyclif's *Dialogus*, see *Mistra Jakoubka ze Stříbra Překlad Viklefova dialogu*, ed. Milan Svoboda (Praha: Česká akademie císaře Františka Josefa pro vědy, slovesnost a umění, 1909).
8. Cited from Malý, "K právnímu odkazu husitství," 210.
9. Ibid.
10. A fascinating study which summarizes similar points regarding the Waldensian movement was written by Amedeo Molnár. See Molnár, *Valdenští: evropský rozměr jejich vzdoru* (Prague: Kalich, 1991).
11. Matthew Spinka, *John Hus at the Council of Constance* (New York: Columbia University Press, 1965), 202.

12. Malý, "K právnímu odkazu husitství," 211.

13. See Vavřinec of Březová, "Husitská kronika," in *Fontes Rerum Bohemicarum* (Prague: Nákladem Nadání Františka Palackého: V komissí knihkupectví Edv. Valečky, 1893), 5:391–395.

14. Říčan et al., *Čtyři vyznání*, 35–52.

15. Palacký, ed., *Archiv český*, 213–216.

16. Ibid., 37.

17. Literally *goods* (symbolizing strength and resources).

18. In the sense of introducing, constituting, and issuing rules for people to follow, thus emphasizing the legal aspect of these four articles.

19. Ibid., 39.

20. Ibid.

21. Ibid.

22. Karel Farský, *Stát a církev: poměr státu českého k církvi římské od prvopočátku až do roku 1924* (Prague: K. Farský, 1924), 46.

23. See Antonín Salač, *Constantinople et Prague en 1452: [pourparlers en vue d'une union des Eglises] Cařihrad a Praha r. 1452: [jednání o církevní unii]* (Prague: ČSAV, 1958).

24. Klaus Schatz, *Všeobecné koncily: ohniska církevních dějin* (Brno: Centrum pro studium demokracie a kultury, 2014), 100–104.

25. František Michálek Bartoš, *Do čtyř pražských artikulů: z myšlenkových a ústavních zápasů let 1415–1420* (Prague: Blahoslavova společnost, 1940), 28.

26. Vaněček, *Dějiny státu a práva v Československu do roku* 1945, 130.

27. Ibid.

28. Ibid., 130.

29. Ibid.

30. An English translation is found in Frederick Heymann, *John Žižka and the Hussite Revolution* (Princeton: Princeton University Press, 1955), 492–497.

31. Malý, "K právnímu odkazu husitství," 211.

32. Ibid., 212.

33. Ibid.

34. As far as I am aware, there is no significant monograph which compares the Bohemian Reformation with its later European counterpart in terms of evaluating the significant and relevant legal issues.

35. Říčan et al., *Čtyři vyznání*, 51–52.

36. Josef Macek, *Tábor v husitském revolučním hnutí*, vol. 1 (Prague: ČSAV: 1956); *Tábor v husitském revolučním hnutí: Tábor chudiny venkovské a městské*, vol. 2 (Prague: Nakladatelství Československé akademie věd, 1955).

37. František Šmahel et al., *Dějiny Tábora* (České Budějovice: Jihočeské nakladatelství, 1988).

Chapter 3

Between the *Four Articles* and the *Iudex Compactatus in Egra*

The Struggle of the Bohemian Diet for the Sovereignty of the Kingdom of Bohemia

From a military perspective, the twelve years between these two respective events were the most crucial of all, as it was not entirely clear whether the intervention of the Kingdom of Bohemia would eventually be able to conquer and exterminate the "Hussite heresy." Hussite factions managed to maintain a cohesive unity despite their differences, a unity only made possible by the existence of their unifying program—the *Four Articles.*

The historical progress of these turbulent years is well known; instead of summarizing this progress, brief consideration will rather be given to enunciating the following: which political forces were present, what their specific aims were, what the eventual results were (in light of the terms offered by these forces), and how all of these were reflected in the constitutional development of the Kingdom of Bohemia.

Following the shameful defeat of the crusader troops at the Battle of Vítkov Hill in 1420, Sigismund proceeded to crown himself as king on the 28th of July in the same year. The circumstances of this shameless act (even though it was still performed according to the old order) were closely analyzed by Bartoš.[1] The ceremony took place at Prague Castle and was led by archbishop Konrád, with many nobles from the Empire and from Silesia in attendance. Conversely, there was only a minimal presence of lords from either Bohemia or Moravia, and no one was present from the town of Prague. Following his coronation, Sigismund proceeded to further dishonor his name by robbing the temple treasury to pay for his army. This vile and disgusting act did not prove to be of any help, however, especially since Sigismund called off the siege of Prague and immediately withdrew. Bartoš described Sigismund's position emotionally and accurately:

> He no longer felt safe near the victorious Prague and withdrew to Kutná Hora in bitter defeat, whereas merely three months ago he had arrogantly dismissed Prague's spokesmen and began marching on the town. He was returning to his fortress as king, albeit a defeated one. Nevertheless, he remained a powerful force of opposition, one that the various generals and statesmen of the revolution would do well not to underestimate, especially given his close ally—the Roman pontiff.[2]

It soon became obvious that these constitutional circumstances could not last long. Sigismund may have been crowned king, but the overwhelming majority of the kingdom did not accept his rule, so he could not exercise his royal power.

At the Diet of Čáslav, which took place in June 1421, Sigismund was deposed, stripped of his succession to the throne, and declared "murderer of the honor and language of the people Bohemia."[3] All factions which agreed with the *Four Articles* of Prague were in attendance at this national diet. Following the defeat of the crusader's army during the summer of 1420, virtually all of Moravia gradually joined the Hussites. Vaněček's summary is a fitting characterization of the state of affairs: from a formal perspective the monarchy was still intact, but in reality the realm had no king; more precisely, it was undergoing a time in between two rulers (*interregnum*).

> The individual Hussite communities and their groups, only loosely bound together, lived a completely independent political life as far as the Bohemian crown was concerned. One might even label such an existence as essentially and actually Republican. Meanwhile, efforts to strengthen the monarchical unity of the state through the institution of a regent had ended in failure. Count Sigismund Korybut (1395–1435) served as governor of the Crown lands twice, but after failing in both cases he returned home to Poland.[4]

Korybut himself deserves a closer investigation from a legal perspective rather than simply a historical one.[5]

The Diet of Čáslav elected a provisional government of twenty people, of which five were lords, four were Prague residents, and the remaining eleven were representatives from various municipalities, including the Tábor municipality. Although temporary, this government was nonetheless quite vital, since for the first time various Bohemian towns were brought to the forefront as the most powerful political agent in the state. One of the more important provisions of the Diet of Čáslav was "that certain rulers and governors have the sovereign power entrusted to them by us together, and no further beyond that; yet when the Lord God grants us to have a king, then each estate mentioned above will maintain their rights and freedoms in accordance with their position."[6]

Even without a king on the throne, no one considered another way of ruling. After all, even the Táborites position was pro-monarchy, with their only preference being that the king should be of native origin. In their view, the lords should prioritize a native-born ruler and should look abroad only if finding a native proved to be futile. The unilateral decision to select a new king without any consideration for the hereditary dynastic claims was truly revolutionary. It took nearly forty years for these efforts to bear fruit, however, even without the efforts of Sigismund Korybutovič (1422–1423, 1426–1427). In modern terms, one could assert that what all of the Hussite representatives wanted was to preserve the integrity of the Bohemian Crown.

It is relatively easy to identify which particular parties were competing in the political arena after 1420. First and foremost, there was the Catholic party led by the emperor and the pope and mostly supported by domestic collaborators. Although there were not too many of them, they abounded throughout the following period, exerting significant influence on foreign intervention. In contrast, the Hussite party was hardly united, but at least had a central program common to all—precisely the *Four Articles*. The radical side was represented primarily by those from Tábor and the Eastern Bohemian union of towns and knights, as well as by the Union of Žatec and Louny. The moderates were mainly from the two Prague towns (the Old Town and the New Town), towns which cooperated with Prague, and majority of the lords and knights. The existence of a unifying program ultimately proved to be the greatest blessing, as there were times when the various Hussite factions fought against each another. Nevertheless, these sides ultimately managed to unite together and act as a greater force against foreign intervention. This is primarily why the Hussite wars were so successful: the ability to quickly overcome their differences and act as a united front against a common enemy became a powerful advantage against their foes. One drawback of this development was that it became rather legalistic, since after every victorious battle the radical side tried to escalate their demands for radicalism, which was unacceptable for the moderate side; they wanted to come to an understanding about further peaceful development with both the church and Sigismund at all costs. This conflict led to the Battle of Lipany on May 30, 1434, where the league of lords led by Diviš Bořek of Miletínek (c. 1360/70–1438) defeated the field troops of the union of Tábor and Orphans. Although this defeat is often described as a disaster, this was not exactly the case in reality. The field troops did lose their position as the decisive political and military force in the country, but moderate Hussites were able to negotiate with Emperor

Sigismund and with the Council of Basel. This eventually led to the end of the civil war in the lands within the Bohemian Crown.

Given the gradual transformation of many of the legal institutions and bodies established after 1420, it is important to observe such developments closely, especially since some of them continued to exist in a constant state. The Hussite organizations can be divided into two primary municipalities based on the vocations or roles played by their members within society. The first included the so-called "field communities"—the armies of those working in the fields. The second included the "domestic towns"—those mainly concerned with the administration of both towns and smaller communities. The basis of the both municipalities was the Estates; both were "communities in the strictest sense of the word, a community of people of the same social standing, tasks, and roles."[7] One could almost say that the Bohemian state became a collective union of all of its individual towns, with the highest decision-making organ being the Diet made up of elected delegates of each community. The Diet would then elect a council of regents whose decrees would become law, supported by the collective power of all municipalities (since the resolution of the Diet was made by the will and command of municipalities).

To realize the significance of this breaking point, one must remember that due to the ongoing revolution, all major judiciary authorities and other administrative authorities presiding over the common folk were defunct at that time.

> Executioners (rural officials) who possessed jurisdiction over criminal law—until then primarily made up of local magnates and lesser lords—completely lost their authority. The various ecclesiastical judicial arms (including the feared inquisition) were absent due to their being purged from the country. As the various nobility and clergymen complained, there was a complete absence of law in the lands.[8]

In truth, the various laws were still "working," so to speak, but in new and different ways which were not so closely under their control. For example, the nobility was no longer the only group in the kingdom organizing diets, since the delegates of towns now also had their own. The new state of affairs naturally meant the creation of new governing bodies unknown in previous times, such as the previously mentioned council elected at the Diet of Čáslav in 1421 (which continued to be renewed again in the following years). Alongside this development came an unprecedented growth of power and influence of both town courts and authorities. Even the nobility saw their usefulness, as they often commissioned them to record important events in the town chronicles. Unfortunately, this legal development has yet to be fully analyzed, and even after forty years one still has to concur with Vaněček's claim that "we are sadly still at the beginning of our efforts to understand this peculiar Hussite legal life and the composition and functions of the Hussite political apparatus."[9] One might easily wonder why such difficulties exist, yet the answer is deceptively simple: it would require the concomitant inter-disciplinary knowledge of legal history, philosophy, philology, history, and theology.

Following the Battle of Domažlice (August 14, 1431), it became increasingly clear that no foreign intervention against Hussite Bohemia would ever succeed. Despite this fact, all sides involved (except the Hussite radicals) were already exhausted by the constant fighting. The external impetus for a certain normalization and proffered solution was the Council of Basel (also called the Council of Basel-Ferrara-Florence), which was convened by Pope Eugene IV (1383–1447). One of its main objectives was to solve the religious and political crisis in the Lands of the Bohemian Crown by reaching a compromise. Similarly, even as it was in 1420, the important legal question arose as to who would be the determinative arbiter between the Hussites and the council. The Hussite delegates assembled together in Cheb in 1432 in order to resolve this issue. It soon became apparent that it was an unsolvable problem from both a theological and a legal standpoint, since Cheb's agreements where the council representatives tried to accommodate the Hussites could not be truly applied to the Catholic side without reneging on the very essence of the agreements themselves. Needless to say, this was entirely unacceptable. What, then, was the ultimate aim of the discussions in Basel? As always, the major issue hinged upon supreme authority and the foundational Hussite principles. The *Four Articles* were meant to be—and indeed, *were*—the main subject matter of the disputation; yet who was to be the judge between the Hussite representatives and their Catholic opponents? Was Scripture or tradition the highest authority?

It is unnecessary to describe every single historical fact linked with the Diet of Cheb, because given the sheer amount of information, this would run contrary to the aims of this work.[10] The most recent work to deal comprehensively with this topic was written by Petr Čornej.[11] From the Catholic perspective, it is clear that the Hussite demands could not be taken seriously, and the fact that the representatives of the council eventually accepted them was an expression of the fact that they were insincere and hoped that in defending the Prague articles, the unity of the Hussite parties would be broken and the influence of Hussitism eliminated. The journal of Petr Žatecký who recorded the negotiations in Basel in great detail is direct proof of such a claim.

The Catholic envoy met with the Hussite representatives in Cheb in order to determine exactly which standard would serve as the deciding factor between the Hussites and the council itself. As is already well known, the negotiations transpired from the end of April to the beginning of May in 1432. Although interesting from both the political and the diplomatic perspectives, the most important concern proved to be their legal and theological value, including the principles which were advocated by the Hussites. The meeting lasted for ten days and the agreement was signed by both parties on the 18th of May in the same year. The agreement has eleven clauses, with the seventh clause being perhaps the most important: it stipulates that in the disputation between the Hussite delegation and the council's theologians "the Holy Scripture, the practices of Christ, the apostolic, and the early church, alongside the councils and teachers truly based on them will serve as the most just and unbiased of all judges."[12] As Bartoš asserts, this was a tremendous victory, but he also rightfully points out that it was only a theoretical success at best.

Why was this essential principle so important, and what exactly did it signify? Scripture, as well as the deeds of Christ and the early apostolic church, were to become the primary criterion for deciding the disputation. At the same time it meant that the Hussites were willing to accept church traditions and all previous council decisions (including various legal norms and the teachings of church fathers and other teachers) so long as they were founded in Scripture, the works of Christ, and the practices of the early church. Unsurprisingly, most provisions made by the pope or the council did not abide by this stipulation, or even outrightly ignored it. The reason for this is rather simple: the council delegates acknowledged one of the main principles of Hussitism—the supremacy of the Bible over any other church authority . . . not just over the pope, but over the council as well. This authority, as Bartoš correctly accentuated, "directly contradicted their conviction that the only true church authority is the council—that is, they themselves."[13] This explains why, from the very outset, the council representatives were convinced that they had only flinched from the demands from their opposition for political reasons and thus did not feel bound by their concession. A contemporary historian evaluated the situation in these terms:

> Their dismissive attitude towards the "Judge of Cheb" became the fundamental principle for how the council continued its dealings with the Hussites all the way up until its closure. All of this remained hidden to the Hussites for a long time in the council's confidential documents and came to light only partially and gradually; however, it quickly started to diminish and obscure any confidence the Hussites might have had towards the council.[14]

It is worth mentioning that theologians were not the only profession involved in the council negotiations, as various diplomats who knew no shame and had no regard for propriety were also present.

As stated in the introduction, the primary aim of this work is not to describe the various historical and political events, as interesting as they might be.

Instead the main focus is on the legal principles presented by the Hussites and formulated rather brilliantly for their time. By no means did the Hussite movement reject the tradition of the church as such; they only exclusively stipulated their acceptance of tradition by demanding that it must be based on Scripture and in accordance with the practices of Christ and the early church. By "early church," we of course understand the institution as it was during the first three centuries of its existence, up until the conversion of Emperor Constantine the Great. Their condition was an indictment of the various excesses and misuses of canon law, the statutes of various popes, and even those of several councils. By stating all of the above, it also became an expression of the pregnant rationale undergirding Jan Hus's courageous actions. It was this perspective on Scripture with which the various representatives of different Hussite factions who advocated the *Four Articles* were completely in agreement as his loyal disciples. Their work could even be viewed as a more lucid formulation of their late teacher's ideals. Almost every declaration of the Bohemian Reformation was intricately concerned with the relation of Scripture and tradition, including the celebrated Bohemian Confession. Nowhere do they refer directly to the Judge of Cheb, however; and even though they deal with the issue in a similar manner, none of their articles is as perspicuous as were those of their predecessors from Cheb.

The paradox of Czech historiography is that aside from one rather Catholic-oriented monograph dedicated to the Compacts of Basel,[15] no major work closely examines the position and distinct message of the Hussite representatives at the council within a broader context. Perhaps even more scandalous is the reality that no Latin protocols were published from these negotiations, despite there being nearly four hundred pages worth of material preserved in the city archives of Basel.[16] The question remains why none of the Czech theologians or historians from this heuristically gifted generation approached the challenge. The only real progress was achieved by František Šmahel, who—aside from revising Krchňák's work from an ideological standpoint—has also attempted to explain the relevant political events and to prepare a future edition of the collection of documents known as the *Compactata*.[17] An important fact is that the Hussites did not ask for peace with the church themselves, as by that time Sigismund still had his sights set on obtaining the Bohemian throne at all costs, and the council was unwilling to budge in their continuous refusal of the *Four Articles*.

The initiative for solving the crisis was offered by the council itself, in the form of a letter of invitation delivered in November 1431 to the Land Diet (since no other authority was available). This invitation was accepted in February 1432, with the diet serving as a negotiation partner to the Church Council. The Judge of Cheb was the first real result of the negotiations, which lasted almost five years until the situation was resolved. Although the main concern here is the entire set of circumstances considered from a constitutional point of view, there is no doubt that a detailed description of certain events (e.g., considered from the viewpoint of the history of diplomacy) is still necessary.

In the so-called Judge of Cheb it was agreed that the Hussites would receive a free hearing at the council with their safety guaranteed. The change of the council's behavior from the earlier case with Hus demonstrates their awareness of the undeniable truth that violence would not prove effective, a fact begrudgingly accepted even by Emperor Sigismund. Therefore, there were no longer any delays to the Hussites' journey to attend the council.

NOTES

1. Bartoš, *Husitská revoluce,* 1:102.
2. Ibid.
3. Palacký, *Archiv český,* 3:228.
4. Vaněček, *Dějiny státu a práva v Československu do roku 1945,* 135.
5. As far as I am aware, no monograph in English dedicated to him. For a somewhat comprehensive article in Czech, see František Bartoš, "Sigismund Korybutovič v Čechách," *Sborník historický* 6 (1959): 171–221; see also the following Polish monographs: Jerzy Grygiel, *Zygmunt Korybutowicz: Litewski książę w husyckich Czechach (ok. 1395 wrzesien 1435)* (Kraków: Avalon, 2016); Jerzy Grygiel, *Życie i działalność Zygmunta Korybutowicza. Studium z dziejów stosunków polsko-czeskich w pierwszej polowie XV wieku* (Wrocław-Warsaw-Kraków-Gdańsk-Lódź: Ossolineum, 1988).
6. Vaněček, *Dějiny státu a práva v Československu do roku 1945,* 135.
7. Ibid., 136.
8. Ibid., 137.
9. Ibid.
10. A detailed description can be found in the second volume of Bartoš's *Hussite Revolution,* as well as in the excellent memorial volume with additions by Czech historians (and in particular the article by our eminent church historian Amedeo Molnár). See Amedeo Molnár, "Chebský soudce," in *Soudce smluvený v Chebu: sborník příspěvků přednesených na symposiu k 550. výročí* (Prague: Panorama, 1982), 2–75.
11. Čornej, *Velké dějiny zemí koruny české,* 5:557–565.
12. Cited from Ibid., 565. For the Latin text of the Judge of Cheb, see František Palacký, ed., *Urkundliche Beiträge zur Geschichte des Hussitenkrieges in den Jahren 1419–1436,* vol. 2 (Prag: Friedrich Tempsky), 282: "*Item in causa quatuor articulorum, quam ut praefertur prosequuntur, lex divina, praxis Christi, apostolica et ecclesiae primitivae, una cum conciliis doctoribusque fundantibus se veraciter in aedem, pro veracissimo et evidenti judice in hoc Basiliensi consilio admittentur.*"

13. Bartoš, *Husitská revoluce*, 2:113.

14. Ibid.

15. Alois Krchňák, *Čechové na basilejském sněmu* (Svitavy: Trinitas, 1997). The first Czech edition of this book came out in 1967 in Rome. See Alois Krchňák, *Čechové na Basilejském sněmu* (Rome: Křesťanská akademie, 1967).

16. This manuscript is held at the University Library in Basel Cod. A I 29. A copy of the entire manuscript was once present in the Hussite Theological Faculty Library of Charles University, but it is currently considered missing.

17. František Šmahel, *Basilejská kompaktáta: příběh deseti listin* (Prague: Nakladatelství Lidové noviny, 2011).

Chapter 4

Land Diets in the Struggle against Sigismund and the Council of Basel

The Journey toward the Compacts of Jihlava (1436)

The diet which was summoned in September of 1432 in Kutná Hora took special note of the negotiations in Cheb, the result of which was deemed as an acceptable outcome. It was also here where the decision concerning who should attend the Council of Basel was reached. The delegation was then given full discretional powers to act in the name and interests of the entire country. The composition of this group is interesting as it showed precisely how much the times had changed since the death of Václav IV. Three representatives from the side of the Hussite-aligned nobility and knights were chosen: Vilém Kostka of Postupice (d. 1436), Beneš of Mokrovous (c. 1400–c. 1464), and Jiří of Řečice. Accompanying them were four burgher representatives: Matěj Louda of Chlumčany (d. 1460), representing Tábor; Písek hetman Laurin of Tábor; Řehoř of Dvůr Králové, representing the Orphan faction; and finally, Jan Velvar (d. 1451), representing Prague. A retinue of priests were also made part of the procession, including such major figures as: Prokop Holý (c. 1380–1434), who was the unofficial head of the entire delegation; the bishop of Tábor, Mikuláš Biskupec of Pelhřimov (1385–1459); Oldřich of Znojmo, the vicar of Čáslav; Markolt of Zbraslavice (d. 1434), a preacher from Tábor; Martin Lupáč (d. 1468), the vicar of Chrudim; Petr of Žatec; Peter Payne (1380–1455), an immigrant from England who was the chief diplomat of the Hussite Revolution; and finally, Master Jan Rokycana, who was spokesperson for both the Prague burghers and the University of Prague (see figure 4.1).[1] The list mentioned here is included primarily to emphasize the sheer diversity of the various representatives and also to demonstrate who held the trust of the entire diet during such crucial times. The proceedings were meant to discuss the *Four Articles of Prague* as previously established in Cheb. In truth, it proved to be much more than a mere discussion, as it represented a major political and constitutional step forward. If a compromise with the church could be achieved and the articles accepted, then nothing would stand in the way of Sigismund's ascension to the Bohemian throne once more (after his humiliating dethronement in 1421). Therefore, even if the goal of the Hussites were to be achieved, it would no doubt give rise to new difficulties, although few were willing to voice such concerns in the face of realizing their hopes for peace. To demonstrate just how seriously the Land Diet considered these proceedings, it is worth noting that the delegation (which had several dozen wagons and was given a full company of horsemen as guards) received military protection—an unorthodox guarantee of safety—for their entire journey from the Catholic entourage of burgrave Zdeslav Tluksa of Buřenice (d. 1433). The delegation left Prague on the first day of December 1432 and returned in May the following year. In addition to the unpublished minutes of the council, the personal diary of one of the delegation members, Petr Němec of Žatec, was published in Czech during the twentieth century, providing a valuable and appealing eyewitness account of the entire process of the disputations.[2]

Instead of showcasing the legal arguments employed by the Bohemian delegation in defense of each article, it should be noted that Jan Rokycana primarily defended communion under both kinds (cf. figure 4.2), Mikuláš Biskupec supported punishing sins, Oldřich of Znojmo advocated the right to preach freely, and Petr Payne argued for the end of the clergy's secular rule. So far, the weighty negotiations did not reach their goal. Following tense negotiations, the Church Council did not present any written position in regards to the *Four Articles*; this meant (as master Rokycana wrote down at the end of the affair) that the Bohemian delegation could not provide any comment on it.[3]

Alongside the returning delegates, the representatives of the Church Council accompanied the Bohemians back to Prague. According to Šmahel,

> their primary goal was to offer and recommend a path of unity (*viam unionis*) to a representative diet of various Hussite sides. As the Hussites could not be expected to actually compromise on this crucial point, the legates were meant to do all within their power to send an entirely new delegation from the Bohemian Kingdom and the Margraviate of Moravia, which would possess the full mandate for Basel to be brought to a close.[4]

The Catholic church representatives ultimately had absolutely no competence to enter into any bargains or treaties with the Bohemian Hussites. If one were to express the purpose of their approximately three months of efforts, their actions could be designated as being subversive. For example, they collected various versions of the *Four Articles* from different sides in order to detect anything that might not be common to all sides and exploit it to undermine the Hussite unity. They also attempted to persuade the more conservative side to abandon the movement, or at least orient themselves against the Hussite radicals. The University of Prague presented their version to the council spokesperson Juan de Palomar (d. 1450), but most of the Utraquist priests were unsatisfied with such a conclusion, as were both Master Rokycana and the Tábor radicals. In the end, the Bohemian Diet brought forward their written version of the *Four Articles* to the delegates of the council on June 22, 1433. This final text was fully in support of what the Bohemian delegation had already presented in Basil. A renowned expert commented on this text with the following remarks:

> If we are searching for the first document which stands at the beginning of all the protracted negotiations concerned with establishing a binding agreement—or more specifically a "compact"—between the Council of Basel and the Diet of the Kingdom of Bohemia, in our opinion it would precisely be this singular document. It probably did not originally take the form of a charter, but it was handwritten by all four Basel advocates of the Hussite articles (i.e., Jan Rokycana, Mikuláš of Pelhřimov, Oldřich of Znojmo, and Petr Payne), with each being responsible for writing down the corresponding article which they were defending in Basel.[5]

Eventually Juan de Palomar ran out of options and was forced to admit to the Diet on June 1433 that his delegation had no true decision-making power. First and foremost, they could not agree with granting the chalice to the laity. The delegates of the council had already tried to approach the various factions of the Bohemian Diet on an individual basis, but they failed. Before their return to Basel, on July 11, 1433, the Bohemian Diet ratified the final and definite version of the articles which would be used by the Bohemian delegation during their second visit to Basel.

The second session of Basel negotiations (from August 11 to September 2, 1433) was held in an even more tense atmosphere than the previous one. The official speech for Bohemia was delivered by Master Prokop of Plzeň (d. 1457), after which Martin Lupáč read and then brought forward the written decision of the Bohemian Diet. Since his version of the text was abridged, the articles were presented in a different order and their impact was lessened as a result. For comparison with the original text (which was already presented earlier), here is its wording:

(1) Firstly, for the communion of the most holy of sacraments to be administered under both kinds, namely bread and wine, to be freely given by the priests to all those who are loyal to Christ in the Kingdom of Bohemia and the Margraviate of Moravia and to their respective peoples.

(2) Secondly, for all who commit mortal sins, especially those of public nature, to be arrested, prosecuted, and punished in accordance with reason and the law of God by those who are entrusted with such a responsibility.

(3) Thirdly, for the word of God to be preached by priests and suitable deacons freely and without restriction.

(4) Fourthly, for the clergy to cease and desist from rulership over any and all secular matters and lands.[6]

It should be obvious that there was an attempt at making concessions from the Bohemian side, since the stipulation was that communion under both kinds would be served only by those belonging to the Hussite Church (thus implying the existence of those faithful who were receiving under only one kind, which was not present in the original *Four Articles*). Another notable change is the absence of a clear demand for all to be punished equally regardless of their position or social standing, which put the entire concept of equality before the law into question and relativized it in a sense. Only the third and fourth (at least in the order above) were abridged without losing part of their original meaning.

The Council of Basel discussed the Bohemian proposal in secret, with the Hussites being informed at the very end that the council would present its proposal in Prague. In the case of punishing mortal sins, the council leaders attacked the wording "by those entrusted with such a responsibility" and demanded that the right to punish should be reserved only for authorized and secular courts. They would also not allow for the free preaching of the word of God without prior approval by an authorized bishop. The salt in their eyes was the prohibition of the secular rule of the church. They responded by proposing a different wording and suggesting that "the clergy must faithfully administer the ecclesiastical possessions of which they are stewards, according to the sacred ordinances of the holy fathers; and the ecclesiastical possessions themselves, other than those entrusted with canonical administration, cannot be appropriated without the offense of sacrilege."[7]

As for the receiving of the chalice for laypersons, in their mind, communion under both kinds was permissible only for lay adults who had already received it thus in the past, with their priests obliged to remind them that Christ is fully present even under only one kind. Since this proposal completely opposed their efforts, the Hussites could never accept such a ridiculous demand. If such a demand were taken seriously, it would ensure that administering communion under both kinds would eventually die out with the death of all those practicing at that time. Unfortunately, the Hussite delegation was never informed of such propositions made behind closed doors in Basel, as they were reserved for the ears of the Catholic delegation alone and meant to be presented at further negotiations at Prague. The Catholic envoy included many famous names of that time: Bishop Philibert of Coutances (1374–1439); Council auditor Juan de Palomar; theologian Heinrich Tocke (1390–1454); and the Dean of Tours, Martin Berruyer (1390–1465). Following their arrival in Prague on October 22, 1433, they received an official celebratory welcome and in the following month presented their proposals to the Land Diet. As was to be expected, their position was met with displeasure and hostility, especially following their statement that three of the articles as they were being submitted had absolutely no right to be changed at all and that the council could further discuss communion under both kinds (i.e., that the issue was still "under" discussion). The situation was not improved by the fact that Palomar brought forward the council's proposal regarding the chalice two days after the proceedings concerned with the other three articles. The Bohemian Diet called for a break in order to have an "inner-circle" discussion concerning the new developments, devising several changes afterward. As far as the chalice for the laity was concerned, there was a call to make Utraquism a requirement even for those areas where people still received under only one kind. The council legates acknowledged the usefulness and salvific benefits of receiving the chalice, but communion under both kinds for children was definitely out of the question. After several days of back-and-forth debate, the council delegates proposed a new version to the Diet, since there was a sincere desire to reach an agreement and conclude the ongoing conflict. It is clear that those who were still on the left side of the Hussite spectrum were far from enthusiastic with the direction in which the negotiations were heading.

The agreement that was meant to be reached between the council legates and the general Diet of the Kingdom of Bohemia and Margraviate of Moravia was originally called *concordata*, but the term was slowly abandoned in favor of the equivalent designation *Compactata* (*Compacts*). Overall, a general agreement was slowly being forged by the end of 1433, although its cost may have been too steep. In the new version of the *Compactata*, the Diet would accept peace and unity with the church and affirm it accordingly in an appropriate manner. In exchange, the chalice for the laity would be permitted for both the Kingdom of Bohemia and the Margraviate of Moravia. If the general Diet accepted the terms for church unity, then the legates would declare official peace with the church, cancel all church interdicts and penalties upon the lands, and publicly order all other Christians to not reprove Bohemian Hussites and instead to consider them as honorable and obedient sons of the church.

The negotiations were difficult and arduous, with another session taking place on November 30, 1433.[8] The latest "package" of objections was expressed by the legates in a comprehensive way: the council would permit the chalice to be received, not out of a position of mere tolerance, but from the authority of Christ and his true bride the church because it is useful and saving. Meanwhile, the other articles were quite problematic, especially the demand for punishment of public sins. Their main concern was whether or not subordinates had the right to reproach or even punish their superiors. Using the works of Saint Augustine to support their arguments, the church delegates claimed that such an event could not happen without public oversight. For the same reason they also denounced theft (most likely aimed at preventing the further confiscation of church property) and killing in God's name. The authority of the laity over clerics might be acceptable in some cases, but only when it was in accordance with canon law. The legates went on to state that all laws should be subject to the law of God, and although they agreed with the Hussites on this matter, they also noted that this could be very hard to achieve in specific legal cases. Regarding the right to preach the word of God freely, they were well aware that many prelates made it impossible for many good preachers to engage in such activities, yet their only response was a recommendation for the individuals involved to appeal their case to a higher authority. The article forbidding the secular rule of priests was met with even harsher criticism, as the church considered selling, pledging, or loaning fiefs as perfectly acceptable actions for clergymen to practice. The only concession was their admittance that some actions were indeed better left to rulers, economists, and economic administrators. There were many loopholes and schemes, and to say that this issue was a complex one would be a gross understatement:

> The legates had problems with the question of whether the coercive power exercised by those officials came from the prelate. The auditor Palomar proved especially evasive in answering such a question; he was eventually forced to present his own opinion, according to which the prelates and other members of the clergy are canonical administrators of all Christ's earthly possessions and as such only tender their jurisdiction and power of enforcement to economists and other officials.[9]

Other issues related to church property did not end there. The legates themselves proved unsure what "church property acquired through just means" even meant, as in their eyes this was where canon law diverged from the practice of the holy doctors. And because there was no clear consensus, they admitted that the Hussite arguments might have merit in the sense that clergymen are mere stewards of earthly possessions and riches but not their lords. The council legates finally acknowledged that in every further matter to be determined the Hussites would conduct affairs according to the Judge of Cheb.

This was followed by a brief closed session where the radicals raised a long list of objections against the compromise. In the end, the Hussites who were assembled agreed to accept the *Compactata* as long as the specific wording toward them was not formulated offensively or in a derogatory manner. On that same day, all of the clergy of the Hussite factions shook hands to confirm their mutual agreement, although at the moment it was only a treaty between the gathered members of the clergy (a kind of "expert" group of the Bohemian Diet); it had not yet been agreed upon by the Land Diet itself. A very important step followed immediately after this agreement, which moved the constitutional development of the Kingdom of Bohemia forward. On December 1, 1433, the moderate Hussite Aleš Vřešťovský of Rýzmburk (c. 1390—1442) was elected by the Diet as provincial administrator, and the *Compactata* were finally completed on the next day. Master Rokycana demanded for the council to issue an official bull supporting the conclusion as insurance and for Palomar to procure peace treaties from the various Catholic lords in the surrounding lands who were still in conflict with the kingdom. Palomar himself made a demand for the Hussites to stop besieging the Catholic-aligned town of Plzeň, but since the town was an official ally of Emperor Sigismund (who was still in open war with the movement), such a demand was impossible to realize. After the bustling negotiations, a deliberate debate on the grounds of the Karolinum took place, and the official final version which took all the legates' objections into account was formulated at last on December 11, 1433. The official recognition of the *Compactata* and its constructive practical implications would still have to wait for almost two years. Originally the Basel legates considered the *Four Articles* as part of the *Compactata*, since they were essentially commentaries on the articles which arose as a result of the long disputations. With all of that having been accomplished, the Diet was expected to formally recognize and ratify the *Compactata*. But when the date for their ratification came, the Land Diet was no longer in any condition to make such decisions since they did not meet the quorum. Many of the Hussites representatives left in disgust, deeming the *Compactata* as too great a concession to make; and to add insult to injury, the legates were informed that the Bohemian Diet would never accept Emperor Sigismund as part of the new peace. A new diet intending to reach a new verdict regarding the fate of the *Compactata* was convened in 1434; the legates themselves thus were not idle and informed the council of the situation in a preliminary report.

Legal historian Vaněček evaluated the proceedings as follows:

> At the diet held jointly for Bohemia and Moravia at the end of 1433, a special provincial administrator was elected to preside over both the Kingdom of Bohemia and the Margraviate of Moravia, alongside a council body of twelve advisors. The full authority of the administrator and the Council was defined rather broadly: to observe and uphold the *Four Articles* (in their truncated

version); to restore law and order within the state, especially when pronouncing judgment or resolving any conflicts or disputes; to act alone and punish rebellion against the law; to appoint judges in all provinces; to levy a special tax on former church property currently in secular hands, as well as a common tax from all property in general . . . to convene the Land Diet at least once per year, with the Diet reserving for itself the right to be the governing body responsible for further negotiations with the Church Council; and finally, to remedy the financial problems and uphold public safety and stability within the country.[10]

From the quotation above, one can clearly see that the Land Diet already maintained an unshakeable position within the country, to the point of exercising administrative and legal power even without a king on the throne. The path toward accepting the *Compactata* would not prove to be easy at all.[11] The legates were still present at the new diet held in 1434. Rokycana sternly reproached them because their promises had never been written down and thus possessed no real value. This garnered a rather aggressive reaction from Palomar, but with no result. Afterward, the university master presented a preface (*praefatio*) of his own to the mutual agreements which had been achieved so far.

Following other eventful debates, the legates urged the Hussite representatives either to accept the *Compactata,* or to send their delegates to Basel once again. At this point it became clear that the church legates had reached the end of their authority, since they could not concede anything further and had to resort to threats which they had no power to carry out. Debates in the diet assembled in order to address the issue of the *Compactata* on January 10, 1434, were among the most stringent to that point. Master Jan Příbram (d. 1448) voted for accepting the agreement in the name of the university, but based on his previous experiences with the council, Master Jan Rokycana was hesitant to agree. In addition, the Diet wanted to expand upon the demands which were to be presented to the council. Then a highly unexpected event happened—an event which appeared from the outside as a manifestation which fully evinced the disunity of the Hussite movement, and in a certain sense later proved to be a disruptive and disintegrating element. The legates were visited by the Rector of University, Master Křišťan of Prachatice (c. 1366–1439), along with six other masters. On behalf of the university, they collectively declared that they accepted the *Compactata* in their entirety. Inasmuch as they considered that their mission had now been accomplished, the legates had no further reason to stay in Prague any longer. The Prague legates left on January 14, but without the actual *Compactata* confirmed by the Diet. On their way back, they stopped in Cheb to release an official document on January 28, 1434, confirming that they had been accepted back into the fold of the church.

A frenzied battle over the *Compactata* later ensued. Martin Lupáč once again went to meet with the council, and despite the difficulty of his efforts, his labor was not entirely without success. The council issued an official bull on February 25, 1434, intended for the provincial governor Aleš Vřešťovský, but for others as well—including lords, burghers of the Old Town of Prague, yeomen, knights, and all towns and communities of the Kingdom of Bohemia. The council issued a command for all to accept the *Compactata* immediately, as well as for all military actions against Plzeň to be aborted without delay. Emperor Sigismund proved himself to be a less-than-useful diplomat and wanted to interfere for his own benefit by trying to include a direct threat in part of the document. Dismissing his demands, the council made it clear to Lupáč that any further demands from the Bohemians to adjust or change the *Compactata* in any way would be ignored.

Although subsequent political developments will not be described in detail in this work, it must be noted that they were indeed a tremendous help in lowering overall tensions, as well as in leading to the eventual acceptance of both the *Compactata* and Sigismund himself. Special reference should be made to the unique chain of events which led to the defeat of the radical Hussites at the Battle of Lipany. The dominance of Hussite radicals was not always viewed in a positive light from the general population. All these circumstances led to an eventual alliance of the Catholic and Hussite nobility which crushed the radical forces at Lipany.

The Diet which gathered in Prague in June 1434 revealed that there was no overall change in relations to the Church Council. Therefore, we cannot claim that the defeat of Hussite radicals changed much regarding how the movement interacted with the Church Council. An official synod of Hussite clergy was arranged for July 25 of the same year (on the feast Saint James). The university masters were conservative in their views, with the notable exception of Master Rokycana, who was more hesitant in his approach. On the other hand, the priests from Tábor were against accepting the *Compactata*, although they had no problems with the *Four Articles* themselves.

The entire situation was quite interesting from a confessional and legal perspective, because the synod was called together by none other than the Bohemian Diet. Although serving as a secular ruling body, here it also participated in ecclesiastical jurisdiction—an element later featured in the German Reformation. This role was accepted more out of necessity than for any other reason since archbishop Konrád, who had converted to receiving the chalice in 1421, died in 1431. And while Rokycana played a major role, he had not yet been elected as an administrator, which explains why the summoning of the General Synod by the Diet was a groundbreaking decision for its time.

To provide a thorough description of the long journey toward the ratification of the *Compactata* by the Estates of Bohemia and Moravia, efforts made by the Bohemian Diet to negotiate with Emperor Sigismund must be included. Based on the Diet's resolution, an official envoy was sent to Regensburg on August 10, 1434. From the side of the clergy, only two people were present: Master Jan Rokycana and Martin Lupáč.[12] At the same time, the Council of Basel sent a message through its own appropriate delegation, led once again by Jan Palomar. Many of the previous legates and bishops who had already negotiated with the Hussites were also present. Although the Catholic representatives had been given the authority only to negotiate with Sigismund, they nonetheless approached the Bohemian Diet in numerous attempts to persuade them into unconditionally accepting the *Compactata*, especially by claiming that the council would make no further concessions.

Sigismund himself did not appear in Regensburg until the very end of August. During their meeting, the Bohemian envoy presented their demands in a very clear manner. The Land Diet was willing to accept mutual peace, but only if it was based on the acceptance of the *Four Articles*, especially communion under both kinds for the Kingdom of Bohemia and the Margraviate of Moravia and for all those who so desired. Rokycana also presented the former amendment to the treaty that was previously discussed in Prague, asking that it be included as part of the peace agreement. As expected, this was met with protests from the council representatives. Following a brief internal consultation to debate the issue, the spokesperson for the Bohemian delegation announced to the emperor that they had full authority to negotiate only with him, not with any of the council representatives.

A curious aspect of these proceedings is that while Rokycana might have been the one in charge of presenting the position of the Bohemian side, as far as actual diplomatic negotiations were concerned, it was the representative of the diet—Lord Vilém Kostka of Postupice—who supervised the actual process. This was no doubt due to the sheer complexity of the negotiations, especially when the Hussites refused to handle the dispute in writing and justified the move by citing a lack of time reserved for the proceedings. Nevertheless, their position was clear, as they directly implored the emperor to adopt communion under both kinds for the land of Bohemia and to exert pressure on the council for the sake of peace. In other contentious issues (the most important of which was communion under both kinds for children), they expressed willingness to debate them further in subsequent councils, provided that Sigismund would help them to be accepted.

The negotiations reached a dead end, as neither of the involved parties was willing to compromise or concede. Even when it finally seemed that an agreement could be reached, Jan Palomar refused to give his written consent, sending the whole process back to square one. Master Prokop of Plzeň's recorded minutes, for which even Palomar himself expressed approval, describe the essence of what happened. In a surprising turn of events, the seemingly never-ending disputation was resolved by complete chance. One of the Hussite delegates happened to meet an unfortunate end and the council legates forbade granting him the honor of a Christian funeral. As a result, the Bohemian delegation announced their return home and that they would submit the entire matter to the Bohemian Diet again. Since the legates of the council were pressing for a specific time-limit of the Diet, the Hussites offered two possible dates, one of which the Catholics agreed with: October 16 (Saint Havel's day), with the resolution being delivered through the town of Cheb some time before November 11 (Saint Martin's day). Overall, the negotiations in Regensburg proved to be ineffectual.

The Land Diet did indeed gather in September, though one week later than originally estimated. One historian notes that

> the emphasis was again placed upon the linguistic, royal, and confessional unity of Bohemia and Moravia during any negotiations with either the Council or Emperor Sigismund, regardless of a separate Moravian *Landfriede* ('territorial peace') led by the chalice-aligned nobility from a month prior (who were concerned primarily with negotiating with Duke Albrecht). At the same time, it seems that the pressure of their circumstances made them open to tolerate the option of having two kinds of faiths in certain areas, but only in places where receiving under only one kind was the norm until that time.[13]

Unfortunately, since written records of the sessions do not exist, a full reconstruction of the events which actually occurred at the Diet is impossible. There is, however, much one can glean from a document sent to Cheb and subsequently forwarded to the council delegates who were still present in Regensburg. The council apparently discussed the issue as early as the end of November, and in early January of 1435 they notified the Bohemian Diet that they would be sending a distinguished delegation to their next meeting with the emperor in Brno.

The Kingdom of Bohemia again consulted concerning the requirements and conditions of Sigismund's succession at what is known as the Saint Valentine's diet, but which was not held until early March 1435. These conditions were drawn up and elaborated by the diet in two separate curia—one intended for the lords, and the other intended for the towns. Although this might seem like another example of fracturing unity, in truth it was the opposite, since the rationale behind the decision was to solve all pressing matters at once and prevent possible misunderstandings. This was accompanied by the fact that the town representatives were often able to understand and name many of the current issues even better than the lords themselves. When paired with the rising importance of towns whose political influence kept increasing until the violent end of the Bohemian Reformation, it should come as no surprise that the town representatives received their own version of the Diet's agreement.

The confession of the *Four Articles* was self-evident, at least in the version which was agreed upon in Prague in 1433; it was already certain that they would be passed. However, ongoing debates concerning their exact wording proved a dilemma which held back their official recognition. The sensitive issue of already-confiscated (and secularized) church property was ultimately neglected in light of more pressing matters, such as the serious demands concerning confessional conditions and relationships in the various provinces. These demands in effect meant the end of the medieval conditions that had prevailed; they would change the shape not only of the church but also the nation. Bishops from Bohemia and Moravia would come to be elected by the Land Diets, forever cementing the church's subordination to the secular estates. In addition, there was a requirement for even the chaplains and advisers of the king of Bohemia to partake in and serve communion under both kinds—a demand which infuriated Sigismund to no end. Additionally, in accordance with the demands of the town curia, the would-be king even had to give his word that he would partake in and serve communion under both kinds himself. This promise, of course, went beyond the various agreements which had been adopted so far. Sigismund further had to agree that he would not invite any monks or priests into the Lands of the Bohemian Crown, nor would he restore any monasteries without prior permission from the town councils.[14]

All these demands outline the reality that while the Land Diet was open to negotiations, it was not willing to budge on the issue of the chalice and other important matters. Despite the urgency of their demands, many Czech historians tend to view these events as a gradual loss of Hussite radicalism, as they consider the movement prioritizing the attainment of peace with the emperor and the Catholic Church over their ideals. However, such conclusions are hasty indeed, mainly due to the clashes and steadfast determination to see the *Four Articles* and other agreements officially recognized and accepted. All the events already described provide an interesting background for better understanding the history of the Czech national law—a worthy topic for study which has yet to be researched to its full potential.

Concerning the tactics of diplomacy employed by the Catholic council, it is of considerable significance to realize that the church did not really wish to address any topic which would inconvenience it in any way whatsoever. The council instructed its legates (who would later negotiate with Sigismund and the delegates of the Bohemian Diet in Brno) to respond only to the demands that were made at the Land Diet in October 1434 and to ignore any new developments, since the church considered the *Compactata* to have already been accepted and thus saw no ongoing reason to engage in further debates.

Also noteworthy is the special mandate issued by the council according to which Bishop Philibert of Coutances was granted a special privilege to exercise any functions canonically belonging to a bishop wherever the legates arrived. Despite all the setbacks, it was becoming clear that reaching an agreement was now close at hand. The Bohemian Estates delegation met with the emperor in Brno on July 2, 1435, with Jan Rokycana as their chosen spokesperson. The Catholic position remained unchanged, as their legates arrived proclaiming that the orally agreed-upon version of the *Compactata* in 1433 would see no further changes. Despite Master Rokycana's best efforts, they managed to uphold such a position throughout the entire duration of the meeting.[15] Before taking a closer look at how the Bohemian delegation fared in their efforts, one rather significant detail must be pointed out: in addition to the six Basel representatives, Albrecht II of Germany (1397–1439)[16] also arrived at the meeting, as well as an official delegation of the Bohemian Hussite Estates and clergy. Although their presence might have served as a disruptive element, an envoy from Tábor composed of Bedřich of Strážnice (d. 1459), Mikuláš of Pelhřimov, and Václav Koranda (d. 1453) also arrived. However, considering the complete seriousness and utter importance of the discussed topics, their arrival proved to be a necessary evil. Several Catholic noblemen such as Jakoubek of Vřesovice (c. 1390–1462) and Oldřich of Rožmberk (1403–1462) made their appearance as well.[17] In the field of jurisdiction, the council's legates proved to be a detrimental and subversive force to the Hussite efforts. Once the bishop of Olomouc, Kuneš of Zvole died (d. 1434), the legates immediately gave ordination to his successor Pavel of Miličín (d. 1450) as bishop. Čornej interprets the situation of the Moravian Catholics with these words:

> Most of the Catholic clergy in Moravia had promised to renew their political and property positions since the arrival of the conciliar message. For this reason, it gave the Ambassadors of the Basel Synod considerable work to convince the Moravian Catholic clergy that the continuing hostility against the Hussites would serve no purpose, considering that all previous military efforts at subjugating them proved disastrous; and since Moravia was a part of the debates to accept the *Compactata*, any agreement reached would include them in its full effect.[18]

Fortunately, there are a plethora of surviving source documents (all originating from the council legates) which help to reconstruct the whole situation. Jean de Tours detailed the entire process for Bishop Philibert, and Gilles Carlier transcribed not only the daily agendas but also any other written documents of note, of which he collected twenty-eight in all.[19] Another Catholic participant named Thomas Ebendorfer of Haselbach (1388–1464) also kept detailed notes, though apparently only for his own personal use.

Master Rokycana held the opening address of the meeting and started with the church legates rather than Sigismund himself. The goal was the same as always: to ask the council to permit the *Four Articles* for Bohemia and Moravia, to expunge the accusation of heresy imposed upon the Kingdom of Bohemia, and to reform the church. The legates, however, remained steadfast in their position and were unwilling to concede anything that went beyond the version from 1433. This was especially true for the additions

> concerning the election of Prague's archbishop and other bishops by persons of secular or spiritual background, restricting ecclesiastical jurisdiction within the Bohemian lands and the prohibition of granting of church offices to foreigners. As Palomar made it clear to the Hussite delegation in no uncertain terms, the Council demanded total submission of the Hussite system to the Church and would not permit any strains that could create any national or area-specific Church.[20]

The council was clearly aware that if they allowed the Hussites to continue it would lead to the creation of a completely autonomous Hussite Church

Figure 4.1   Archbishop Jan Rokycana from Schedel's Weltchronik in 1493. *Source:* Hartmann Schedel, *Die Schedelsche Weltchronik* (Nürnberg: Anton Koberger, 1493), fol. 241v. Credit: Jan Blahoslav Lášek.

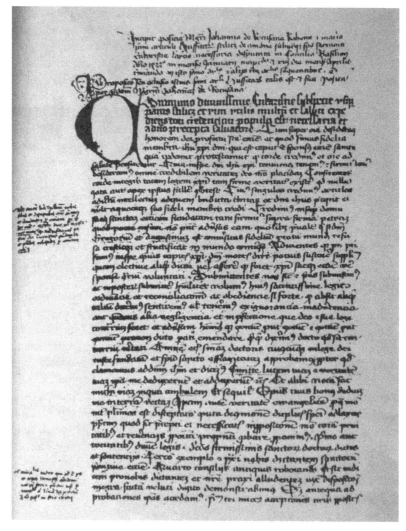

Figure 4.2 The Beginning of Jan Rokycana's Speech at Basel Concerning Communion in Both Kinds (Jan. 16, 1433). The Marginal Notes Were Written by Nicholas of Cusa by His Own Hand. *Source*: St. Nikolaus-Hospital, Cusanusstift, Bernkastel-Kues, Cod. Cusanus 166, fol.1r. Credit: Jan Blahoslav Lášek.

which would be beholden only to the secular estates. As Palomar stated it, any "unity" of this sort would be nothing more than mere fiction. The council also demanded that communion under both kinds be restricted to those who were already accustomed to such practices. This effectively meant that once the current generation died out, there would be no one left to continue the practice, and thus the problem would be solved. The article concerned with

the secular rule of priests also came under heavy fire, as the council representatives insisted that church goods were not to be detained by any secular
persons or institutions, whereas the Hussites protested by claiming that the
church goods should not be detained *unjustly* rather than never at all. The
Hussite interpretation meant that in cases involving a

> competent secular authority, the seized or pledged ecclesiastical possessions
> may be held fairly. The revolutionary seizure of ecclesiastical goods would
> therefore be legalized and the hope of its future restitution, and thus any chance
> of future church restitution and strengthening of the political and economical
> influence of the institution, would be reduced to a minimum.[21]

Both sides could agree on the declaratory statute (i.e., enforcement power)
attached to the *Compactata*. The church legates declared that they were not
authorized to discuss any possible changes regarding the *Compactata* and
thus could not address any of the Hussite's proposals without receiving new
instruction from the council.

Once Sigismund saw that the negotiations between the Hussites and the
council might be successful and that the chalice was going to be permitted, he
made his own daunting move. Blinded by his greed for the Bohemian crown,
on July 6, 1435, the emperor promised the Hussites that he would keep the
territorial ties to the chalice for the laity without consulting the church legates
first. In other words, wherever communion under both kinds already existed,
it would continue to be served. This was not the only promise the king offered
to the Hussite delegates. He promised that he would issue an official charter
containing his consent to the election of the archbishop of Prague and his
suffragans and that the election would be carried out by a committee comprised of representatives from both secular and spiritual estates. This was a
major interference with existing canon law, the confessional law, and the
even constitutional law. According to the corpus of ecclesiastical law, the
appointment of bishops and archbishops was always done by the correspond-
ing church chapter and then confirmed by the pope. The situation in the Lands
of the Bohemian Crown was much more complicated, however, since "their
chapters primarily respected their liege lords, who often proposed their own
candidates for the position."[22]

The council sought a different approach: to send its legates to the Hussites
as administrators, while the pope would later appoint his own bishops. The
suggestion received a resounding rejection from all Hussite parties. On July
6, 1435, Sigismund issued another official privilege in favor of the Hussites,
one which stipulated that only Hussites could become members of the town
councils. A similar arrangement was included for the position of royal cham-
berlain, as it should be also be filled by a Hussite Prague burgher. Catholics

were to be allowed within Prague and its allied towns only with consent from the community. The emperor ordered the monks and canons not to interfere with any Utraquist ecclesiastical administration, as well as not to insult or offend people who received communion under both kinds. This order was enough to make the council legates nervous. A separate meeting on July 14, 1435—without the council representatives present—even went one step further and represented a significant encroachment on the constitutional law: consent to an addendum to the adoption formula of the *Compactata*. Its importance lies in the fact that

> it contained a stipulation that the Compacts could never be used to impinge upon the freedoms and privileges of the Kingdom of Bohemia and the Margraviate of Moravia. Therefore, the *Landrechte* (i.e., customary laws of the land), as both Sigismund and the Hussite delegation understood them, would become the norm superior to the Compacts themselves. This was perfectly in harmony with how both the emperor and the Hussites imagined the superiority of secular power over ecclesiastical power.[23]

The wording was completely unacceptable for the council officials and is found nowhere in the final text of the agreements, although it was actively practiced. Sigismund came under fire from the Catholic delegation over this issue, but ultimately his aim was to ascend the throne rather than obey the church, so he had no reason to listen to their complaints. However, before this entire legal and political drama (which began in Cheb in 1432) could ultimately reach its denouement, the final act of the drama would include even more arduous negotiations and peripeteia. One of these decisive changes came to realization at the turning of the year 1435/1436 in *Székesfehérvár* in the Kingdom of Hungary.

Although the primary concern here is the legal history and development of the Kingdom of Bohemia, it is important not to omit historical events which may not have been legal or constitutional in their character, but which had an underlying influence on the history of Czech politics and law. One such event was the appointment of Master Jan Rokycana as archbishop of Prague along with two other ordained bishops on October 21, 1435, at the Diet on Saint Matthew's Day. The oral agreement with Sigismund notwithstanding (see above), the Diet lacked written authorization to make this appointment. The new archbishop was not appointed by the plenum of the Land Diet, but rather by a committee of electorates (who in turn were appointed by the Land Diet). The following list represents the members of this committee. There were eight persons from a secular background: Lord Menhard of Hradec and Lord Hynce Ptáček of Pirkštejn (1404–1444), lower nobility members Diviš Bořek of Miletínek and Havel of Dřevěnice, the burghers Jan Velvar and Pavel

Dětřichovic, Ambrož of Kutná Hora (former mint-master), and Master Václav
of Sušice; there were eight members of the clergy: the Prague priests Pavel
of Slavíkovic of Saint George, Václav of Lužnice of Saint Nicholas, Mikuláš
Řehlovec of Betlém and Jan of Saint Stephen, along with Vít of Kutná Hora,
Oldřich of Znojmo (vicar of Čáslav), Bartoš of Louny and Ondřej of Sušice.[24]
All of them unanimously voted for Rokycana to become the new archbishop.
The two bishops appointed at the same time were Martin Lupáč and the priest
Vaněk of Vysoké Mýto. The constituency of the committee of electorates
reveals the primary legal criteria at play: diversity and representation from
various estates and regions. Overall, this was a major breakthrough in terms
of both canon and state law, since the voter responsible for appointing clergymen was neither a church chapter nor a territorial lord, but instead the state
itself! There is no better demonstration of how the position and power of the
state shifted. This also shows who bore the true decision-making power, even
to the point of overriding norms and changing current practices which were
valid until that time. One cannot underestimate the importance of this serious step forward since it made clear that the legal developments could not be
hindered or repelled in any way. A major witness of this turning point was
Sigisimund's chancellor, Kašpar Šlik (c. 1396–1449), who could report to the
emperor about the dominant joyful atmosphere that was reigning in Prague,
but also about the first appearances of the Hussite ultra-conservative forces
against Rokycana and his suffragan bishops.[25]

To say that the council fathers were taken aback by the archbishop's unauthorized appointment would be an understatement. One can easily agree with
the remarks made by Čornej that this election gave a clear signal concerning
the future direction of the Calixtine Church to the national and state churches.
Supposedly, it would have been only natural if the Moravian Hussites also
threw their support behind Rokycana. The news about what had happened in
Prague took a long time to reach the ears of the council, who self-assuredly
continued to debate their own agenda. In their mind, the Hussites should abandon any other addenda beyond what had already been written down in 1433,
since they would never have approved of them anyway. They also demanded
an affirmation that no one would be forced to follow the *Compactata*.

The last session of negotiations before the *Compactata* were finally
adopted (which, as noted above, also included other legal actions such as
accepting Sigismund as King of Bohemia) took place in *Székesféhérvár*[26] at
the very end of 1435 and on January 11, 1436. The council wrote directly
to Sigismund and warned him that he was incompetently interfering with
ecclesiastical-legal questions and condemned his separate dealings with the
Bohemians. Having made their position clear, the Catholic Church considered it obvious that no further amendments could be expected, a decision

which resulted in both the movement and the emperor ignoring the will of the council altogether.[27]

In regards to the negotiations which took place in the Kingdom of Hungary, it is important to take into account that the Bohemian Diet (i.e., Hussite) delegation was comprised of eleven members, but there were no members of the clergy among them. Although the delegation was official, it did not possess written authorization from the Diet. Due to the extremely complex nature of the situation, the Prague Diet purposely did not provide them with authorization in order to prevent any possible insinuation that they had been forced in any of their decisions. As things stood, it was clear that the *Compactata* would not be officially accepted. It was unfortunate that Jan Rokycana did not participate this time; but given his new position, perhaps his absence actually prevented more conceivable problems, since it would have been quite difficult for all parties diplomatically. The chosen spokesperson for the Hussite delegation was Jan Velvar, an Old Town of Prague burgher and an Utraquist. Based on what one can glean from the surviving records, he was certainly vigorous in his negotiations, but not in an excessively diplomatic manner.[28] In response to the gathering, Juan de Palomar suggested to the emperor that he should sign a charter where he would commit to refrain from interfering in any matters concerning the faith or the power of the church; and if he had already decided or expressed himself on such matters, then he should declare that any agreements or concessions were achieved through underhanded and fraudulent means.[29] The emperor met with his advisory council and quite possibly even with the Bohemian delegates, but did not confirm the agreement in its proposed form. He promised to confirm only the first section of the general version of the *Compactata,* to uphold them, and to protect against their distortion. Overall, there was a general tendency between the Hussites and Sigismund to reach an agreement, which was ironically only further strengthened by the constant attempts of the church to interfere. At last Sigismund proceeded to take concrete action at the final session of negotiations: he issued an officially signed writ guaranteeing the Hussites all the religious freedoms which he had previously promised them on July 6, 1435. This signed document is generally called the *emperor's compact (compactata cum imperatoris facta)* in scholarly literature. Its general purpose was to expand and supplement the church's unconfirmed compact.

In addition to the demand for the chalice to be tied to specific territories and for the creation of a registry of Utraquist vicarages, the emperor also agreed that church benefices within the Hussite Church should not be granted to foreigners. Moreover, no native citizen of the Kingdom of Bohemia and the Margraviate of Moravia was to be prosecuted and judged for belonging to the Church when venturing outside of their borders; the elected metropolitan bishop of Prague and his suffragans were to be appointed by a combined vote of the Estates Committee and the clergy; all priests of the Prague archdiocese were to be subordinate to their appointed metropolitan, and the metropolitan was to ordain priests under one kind and also under both kinds, as well as for the same to be done by the bishops of Litomyšl and Olomouc, whose duty was to serve communion from the chalice to those who so requested it.[30]

Sigismund pledged not only to observe all these promises but also to ensure that these rules were adopted by the council and the pope. Though Sigismund was Catholic, he was also a scheming monarch, and anything that he could exploit to achieve supremacy over the church was well within his interests to enforce—even if it meant legitimizing the outcomes of the Hussite Revolution. It simultaneously opened the way to Prague. The charter was an important message to the council and to the Catholic Church as a whole in the sense that the secular ruler of the Western world acknowledged the political and constitutional reality of the Kingdom of Bohemia and the Margraviate of Moravia. Even more so, he did not want to change anything, and he defended the principle of the superiority of secular power over ecclesiastical power. Historian Petr Čornej speculated whether this was a result of political pragmatism and driven by a desire to finally gain the Bohemian crown or more of a long-term effort to unite Central Europe under a single ruler for his future successor. He reached the conclusion that in all likelihood Sigismund, as a talented statesman, realized that the political situation and internal structure found in the individual states of Central Europe had changed since the end of the fourteenth century. He realized well enough that the sovereign position of the ruler was also shifting, so he abandoned the notion of exterminating the Hussites by the sword. Although enough detail is known about him to demonstrate that he did not care for ideals, Sigismund's greatness rested in the fact that he could not overlook the influence and power wielded by the various estates; and if he could not destroy their hold over the state, then the only remaining option was to share power with them if he wanted to rule at all.

If at the beginning of the revolution he cared mostly for the opinions of high nobility, following the Battle of Lipany he had to make peace with the fact that at least some of his future partners in power would be lower nobility and representatives of royal towns. This indisputable foresight ranks Sigismund as one of the greatest statesmen of the late medieval period and a dignified heir of Charles IV.[31]

The negotiations of Hussite delegates at all their meetings (even after Lipany) proves that despite their many setbacks, they were able to lead the Hussite struggle to a victorious end through peaceful means. The moderate Hussites who led these negotiations were not traitors in any measure, but instead saviors of the movement's ideals and efforts, given that they succeeded in realizing those ideals in the long term. They were also pioneers of a new definition of state and law.

The council legates suggested that the final act of this drama should take place in Prague, but this proposal was impossible since the Hussites demanded that the emperor first accept the *Compactata* and their other demands before he could be declared king of Bohemia. Following a brief diplomatic endeavor, it was decided that the final act would take place in the Catholic town of Jihlava. The proceedings of the Land Diet which transpired there between June 6 and July 5, 1436, had a tremendously important impact on the political, ecclesiastical, and legal history of the Kingdom of Bohemia. One the one hand, they demonstrated that the Roman Church was only able to act when forced by circumstances; and on the other hand, that the church was not very serious about it. A notable example of this is when the council legates declared that they did not have the authority to confirm the appointment of an archbishop and his suffragan bishops nor could they grant them ordination. This declaration happened in spite of the fact that this issue was one of the Hussite conditions (one they unfortunately had to relinquish) for accepting the validity of the *Compactata*. This "severe wound" to the Hussites prevented the Utraquist Church from ever becoming fully stable until its very end in 1622. Unlike the Unity of the Brethren (*Unitas Fratrum*), the Hussite Church never denounced the classical ordination of its priests in accordance with canonical law, not even during the sixteenth century when many other churches emerging from the German and Swiss Reformation popularized the notion. As a result, the Hussites always had to struggle with gaining ordination for its priests in foreign lands. Still, the conclusion of the constitutional development which originated from the Hussite Revolution centered on the acceptance of the *Compactata* and Sigismund as the king of Bohemia. Although many Hussite towns originally insisted on the ordination of the archbishop and bishops as a condition, they eventually relented and agreed to accept the *Compactata* even without them. The extent to which this was a prudent decision remains an ongoing debate, but the lands were exhausted from war and did not have the strength to continue fighting; even the aging emperor desired peace. Thus, the Catholic legates remained the chief obstacle to achieving peace, especially since they were persistent in their efforts to mitigate the impact of the *Compactata* on church life and society as a whole as much as possible. For example, they tried to limit the importance of the *Compactata* only for Bohemia, despite the fact that the Moravians also participated in the struggle for their realization and even had their own representation in Jihlava (though this latter was weak and lacked the full authoritative power normally granted by the Moravian Diet). In the end, the Hussite diplomats persuaded the legates to include the Moravian Margraviate in the ecclesiastical-political agreement under preparation. However, they did not assert the jurisdictional rights of Archbishop Rokycana over the Moravian Calixtines, thus leaving them subordinate to the functional diocese of Olomouc. Above all, there was one major legal issue which had to be solved immediately: the question of who would serve as the representative parties to officially agree with the *Compactata*. The official formulation stated that it would be between *the legates of the holy Council of Basel and the General Diet of the Kingdom of Bohemia and the Margraviate of Moravia.*[32] Yet this is factually incorrect because Emperor Sigismund and the Moravian Margrave Albrecht II of Germany also added their seals. Its actual wording was more important, since it was the same version which had been agreed upon on November 30, 1433, in Prague, although it included the declaratory charter that originated from the meeting in Brno in July 1435. Two pertinent questions remain: first, how were the *Compactata* adopted? Second, which new circumstances did they bring forth and effect in terms of legal status? Regardless of their particular form, the main advantage of the *Compactata* was that the Hussites were once more united with the Western Church, which was in the best interest of both parties concerned.

Unlike many churches that arose later during the Reformation, the Hussites never had any intention to exist completely independent of the universal reality of the Western church. Their demands were originally meant to be implemented for all Christians, and only when that proved to be impossible did they concede to become a particular church with its own orders. This motive explains why the Hussites were pleased when the *Four Articles* were eventually adopted at all, even if only in their more moderate form. As already mentioned, as far as preaching the Gospel and punishing mortal sins were concerned, an agreement concerning their moderate version was already accepted back in 1433. Concerning the rulership of the church over goods (i.e., secular property or lands), eventually the opinion of the Bohemian legal tradition prevailed, asserting that priests are mere stewards (*administratores*), never lords (*domines*) of such domains.[33] Communion under both kinds was accepted to be on equal grounds with communion under one kind. This is clearly demonstrated in the declaration that "his body is not present solely under the species of bread, nor is his blood present solely under the species of the wine, but Christ is equally and fully present under both species."[34] The final agreement was that clergymen in both Bohemia and Moravia could serve communion under either one kind or both kinds, and communion was both useful and salvific for those who practice receiving from the chalice. The Hussites did fail to achieve children being allowed to receive from the chalice because the council would only permit people of reasonable age (i.e., adults) to receive under both kinds. The article concerning the laity receiving the chalice was a hard pill for the council to swallow. The Hussites were dissatisfied with the solution of communion for children, and in the future they attempted unsuccessfully to agree with the council on this critical issue. The arrangement against children receiving communion would persist throughout the movement's history despite numerous efforts at changing this state of affairs. One major problem remained which posed a possible threat to the recently closed agreement: the pope himself did not endorse the *Compactata*. His disapproval would cause many great controversies in the future and would amplify yet more moments of crisis.

Originally the *Compactata* were meant to have been signed on July 3 on the town square in Jihlava. However, due to many issues surrounding both protocol and procedure which were necessarily considered a priority, the actual ratification took place two days later on July 5, 1436 (cf. figure 4.3). The focal point of the ceremony comprised the mutual exchange of the *Compactata* signed by both sides. For the Hussites this role fell to Jan Velvar, a burgher from Old Town of Prague. Alongside the *Compactata*, he also provided the council legates with a declaratory charter by all Hussites to uphold unity, tranquillity, and peace with all of Christendom. Representatives of the Bohemian Diet and selected Utraquist priests then took an oath of allegiance to the universal church at the hands of legate Philibert. All of them, of course, then shook hands with Jan Rokycana to symbolize their conscientious acceptance of his role as their archbishop. Despite all the pomposity and pageantry surrounding the whole event, it was apparent that tensions were still running high. At the end of the ceremony, Rokycana read the official order given by the council's legates which commanded all Christians to maintain peaceful relationships with both Bohemia and Moravia. It was explicitly stated that Moravian bishops were to serve communion under both kinds, and no one was allowed to censure the Hussites for receiving the chalice. In an ironic and paradoxical turn of events, the long-sought peace was declared in the Catholic town Jihlava, where most of the population spoke almost exclusively German.

The subsequent Catholic worship service (where communion was celebrated under one kind) was held in the parish church with the emperor as an honored guest. When evening arrived, fires were burning and bells were ringing in celebration of the agreement which had finally been reached. The next day would already prove to be a trial by fire in itself, since it was the day dedicated to honor Master Jan Hus; exactly twenty-one years had passed since his burning at the stake in Constance. Fortunately, everything still progressed smoothly. Following the official reading of the Bohemian Land

Figure 4.3 Plates with the Compactata from the Mid-Fifteenth Century. After the Conclusion of an Agreement with the Basel Council, the Plates Were Exhibited in the Now Abolished Corpus Christi Chapel in the New Town district of Prague. It Contains a Written Affirmation that Those Who Receive Communion in both Kinds are Faithful Members of the Church. *Source*: Lapidarium, National Museum in Prague; photo repr. Ota Halama, "Osudy kaple Božího těla po roce 1437," in Staletá Praha 29/2 (2013). Credit: Jan Blahoslav Lášek

Diet's position by Master Petr of Jindřichův Hradec (identified as Master Petr of Mladoňovice according to Čornej), the main *ceremonial* was concluded peacefully, but one important matter remained to be resolved. The moment had now arrived for the paramount discussion concerning the terms under which Sigismund would be accepted as king of Bohemia.

Though he was an experienced politician, the emperor was not a man of high moral character, and his behavior at the events surrounding his acceptance as king was clear proof of this assessment.[35] It also proves the main thesis of this work concerning the transformation of the Bohemian state into the Estates. He was fully willing to accommodate the estates and towns in any capacity whatsoever, just so long as he was guaranteed the privilege of sitting on the throne. It was common knowledge that he hated Master Jan Rokycana. Thus, when the time came to promise the Bohemians that they could appoint their own archbishop, he callously replied that it mattered nothing at all to him who held the position, even if they were to choose a monkey. On July 13, 1436, he was forced to issue an official edict which was more than slightly controversial regarding the current canon law, since both his opponents from the Estates and the town representatives demanded it. The edict declared that the right of the royal election of the archbishop of Prague was thereby being transferred to the Bohemian Estates. At the same time, it also confirmed the validity of Rokycana's appointment along with the two other bishops who were elected. Due to his royal rights and privileges, the king's word carried substantial weight in such times, and Sigismund was undoubtedly aware of this fact. In all likelihood, he was already convinced of a fail-safe: the near certainty that Rokycana would not receive ordination as archbishop.

On July 20, 1436, Sigismund issued another important edict regarding the *25 Articles* addressed directly to the various Bohemian Estates, with a similar edict also being sent to various town councils.[36] Bartoš was correct in calling it a "brilliant achievement of diplomatic cunning."[37] It was essentially a formal and political capitulation which affirmed the specific freedoms of the Bohemian Estates, but in exchange the Estates were obligated to honor him as their *true heir and natural lord*. By confirming the document, the Bohemian Estates formally recognized the heredity of the throne, and thus surrendered their right to possess any clout in the election of future monarchs. At first glance, it may seem that the constitutional situation of the state was reverting to how it had been before the outbreak of the revolution, but that is a mistaken assumption. Some of the Estates' demands formulated earlier (e.g., that the king himself would receive under both kinds, or that he would have two Utraquist chaplains on his court) were silently ignored. On the other hand, the Hussites managed to achieve many of their confessional, national, and economic demands. For example, the royal towns were made exempt from taxes from 1419 onward, and any interest on Jewish loans was canceled from the same year. Sigismund bypassed many of the demands by claiming that they would be addressed in the state council which was yet to be created. Bartoš described this maneuver as follows:

This council, which was supposed to be the primary constitutional guarantee of the emperor's rule and government, is mentioned at least five times in the registry, though never without a noticeable hint of irony, all the while tacitly striking out those demands which depended on the towns the most in order to ensure that their rule would not fall to anyone who is a hetman and would not concede self-armament to them. The towns were eventually abandoned by the other two estates and had to accept their loss—a loss only somewhat tempered by the privilege that guaranteed safety from burghers who were exiled or expelled during wartime.[38]

Sigismund also came into conflict with the Estates regarding castles of the Crown which were previously confiscated by the various lords and knights, none of whom were keen on returning them. Those who even entertained the idea demanded compensation from the confiscated church properties in exchange. The Bohemians were similarly unwavering concerning their next demand for Sigismund to be accepted as king at the next Land Diet to be convened in September in Prague since the emperor had not yet returned the coronation insignias and *Zemské desky* (*Landtafel*).[39] Sigismund was afraid that in the meantime, the Estates might reconsider their amenability to accept him as their ruler or that Prague would be occupied by one of his enemies—both scenarios which he wanted to prevent at any and all cost. At his suggestion, the Jihlava Diet was postponed for two weeks while he hurriedly sent for both missing items to be delivered.

The final celebration of the official reception of Sigismund as king took place in Jihlava on August 14, 1436. Aleš Vřešťovský resigned as provincial governor, the spokesman for the Bohemian Diet was Menhard of Hradec, and Old Town burgher Jan Velvar became the spokesman for the various towns. The lords, the members of the lower nobility, and the representatives of twenty-five Bohemian towns swore an oath of loyalty to their king, though accompanied by one last mutual compromise which the Bohemian side accepted. Although Sigismund became king, he was not given a new official coronation; instead his previous coronation, which was unjustly performed by the emperor shortly before his defeat at the Battle of Vítkov on July 28, 1420, was tacitly recognized as being valid. The Crown lands finally experienced peace again, but only to a certain degree. Several towns—Tábor, Kolín, Stříbro, and Hradec Králové—negotiated with Sigismund separately, but they did not attend the Jihlava Diet, nor did they accept Sigismund as their king; discussions with them would take place in the near future. From a legal perspective it is important to note that on August 16, 1436, the emperor declared—already as king of Bohemia—peace between Bohemia and the other nations.[40] He later set out on a triumphant journey to Prague, actually arriving on August 23, 1436. He renounced himself and entered the Church of Our Lady before Týn, where he was welcomed by Jan Rokycana. There could be no better characterization of this account than the explanation offered by Bartoš:

> The cunning deceiver had at long last captured the greatest fortress of the kingdom, and could now spend over a year continuing his systematic and deliberate act of retaliation for having suffered so many sacrifices and so many years of effort. This was the main focus of his activities during the next fourteen months which he spent in his home town, a place which he was eventually forced to abandon in fear of rebellion by those whom he had deceived and betrayed, only to meet the end of his ignoble life a mere month later at the border of the Bohemian state.[41]

Although Bartoš was more concerned with ethics and morals, he is nonetheless correct in his assertion that Sigismund was a great and gifted ruler. Another scholar describes the Jihlava Diet by stating that the turbulent history of the Hussite Revolution had come to an end even as history continued marching forward.[42]

In order to grasp the details of some of the subsequent and momentous legal events such as the acceptance of future rulers after Sigismund (i.e., Albrecht the Magnanimous from 1397 to 1439 and especially Jiří of Poděbrady from 1458 to 1471), a comprehensive characterization of the entire period of the Hussite struggle for a new Bohemian state up to the year 1436 will be provided based on available legal literature.

Assuming that one dismisses some of Vaněček's more radical expressions and blatantly ideological viewpoints, his other opinions and judgments are interesting and even correctly asserted. It is an indisputable truth that from a legal and constitutional perspective, the consequences of the Hussite Revolution were enormous. For a very long time a ruler was actively prevented from assuming the throne or taking independent action (something that only truly presented its own problem under the House of Habsburg). The rule of magnates came to an end and has never returned. The changes that were accomplished through the strength of the united Hussite movement and its armies paved the way for a new type of Estates monarchy—one which experienced a much closer relation between the monarch and the secular Estates. Unfortunately, this monarchy of the estates was prevented from developing further due to the eventual rise of the intolerant approach of the Counter-Reformation. The political power of the clergy (which was one of the triggers behind the revolutionary changes) vanished from the Crown lands for a long time, along with any ecclesiastical-feudal lords. The property of the church came into the possession of the nobility and towns and become secularized as a result.

Vaněček saw the Hussite Revolution as foreshadowing (or perhaps even as a precursor of) later European Revolutions which helped erase the feudal order of society between the sixteenth and eighteenth centuries. He is not wrong in his assumption, as the collective goal of all these movements was to liberate human beings and even society as a whole from every "bond and chain" which would enslave the individual. There was a radical transformation of relationships in society throughout this era.

As far as the Bohemian state was concerned, the bourgeoisie of the roughly thirty important towns in the land (led by Prague) managed to become such a powerful and influential force in the state during the early phase of the movement that they were *the* primary decision-making body in the entire state. Even if they did not manage to maintain the position of hegemony in the long term, they were forevermore seen as an equal force next to th nobility itself. The patriciate was subsequently never the sole holder of power in our towns again. On the contrary, they were replaced by a new and strong social group. At the same time, lower class nobility gained equal standing with the magnates-nobility.[43]

Every comparison of this sort is complex, raises a number of questions, and perhaps might even inspire doubts as to whether it is even possible at all; yet there is a possible comparison to be made with the German and Swiss Reformations, although their own transformations of the state (i.e., duchies and cantons) were much more gradual and not interrupted by force. Questions concerning nationality also belong the history of state and law, as briefly mentioned in the introduction. The Hussite movement was certainly not intolerant regarding nationality, because many German Hussites worked and had an influence in both Bohemia and in foreign lands alike—many of whom paid for their conviction with their own lives (e.g., Nicholas of Dresden). Petr Payne (also call Peter English in Bohemia), a highly important diplomat of the Hussites, came from England.[44] The German patriciate in towns was an entirely different matter. This German patriciate was highly conservative and associated with both the king and with high church circles. This inevitably led to their position in Hussite-aligned towns becoming unstable and uncomfortable. Some left voluntarily of their own accord while others became politically engaged against the movement and were exiled as a result (though this was not due to their nationality). Vaněček provided an interesting commentary on the matter:

> The German patriciate, whose activities so far had either a German or mixed character, disappeared from all of the towns of the Bohemian state's center [i.e., from Bohemia and Moravia]. The German character was also greatly weakened in the peasant colonization settlement along the frontier zones. The Germanization of high nobility vanished, just as foreign influence was uprooted in the high prelates formerly rich monasteries and at the University of Prague.[45]

Overall, the Hussite movement certainly contributed to the formation of the nation-state both within the local and European context. Christian universalism (internationalism) had long shrouded the continent and cloaked the various problems that plagued feudal Europe for centuries. But from the second half of the fourteenth century onward, this vision was no longer sufficient. Vaněček also commented that

> the Hussite movement acquired an international, pan-European significance in helping to develop the contradictions that existed in the so-called "Roman Empire." In particular, the Hussite movement revealed the contradiction between the conception of the Empire as a universally Christian political society

and the Empire as a factional German community. The inchoate Bohemian state began to clearly design itself as a Bohemian state of the later feudal nationalities.[46]

This corresponds with the essential notion that the restoration of the lands to their previous legal condition became impossible after 1436, even if it might not have been so obvious at first. The feudal government was restored, but it was also entirely different. Even the form of this restoration was not the same, and there was simply no returning to the state of affairs in 1419 (or 1415). Many substantial changes occurred which reflected everything found within the progressive goals of the Hussite Revolution. The economic and social conditions of society were also permanently altered. It is certainly not easy to summarize all of these shifts and developments in just a few short pages, but Vaněček's words will serve as a helpful and accurate synopsis: "The most obvious novelties were precisely in the old aristocratic institutions of state law, in the composition and competence of the Diet, in the appointment and functions of the highest provincial authorities, in the military legal organization (regions and their leadership) and even in town administrations."[47]

For all of the diversity of the Hussite parties, we can generally claim that the Hussite communities were certainly educated and well-cultivated. The changes that the Hussite movement brought for the benefit of the lower nobility and bourgeoisie became firmly enshrined in the law. They were established out of necessity, since otherwise they would not have survived even for a single generation. In addition, everything was written down and recorded: resolutions of the Diet, findings of the Provincial Court, and royal (or rather administrative) ordinances. Another intriguing fact is that the lower nobility acquired an interest in becoming an active agent in enforcing the law. In 1435, before the arrival of Sigismund, they demanded "that lords, knights, and squires of every region would be represented at the diets and in the land registers. For during the times of King Václav, when only the lords had representation at the diets, many people were oppressed."[48]

These changes show the specific direction in which state law was heading. The strife and disputes between the nobility and the towns which would soon be created were a natural consequence of the bourgeoisie's growing influence. It reached its peak during the revolution, with the bourgeoisie not willing to relinquish their newfound political power. Although the post-Hussite times saw a rapid decline of this power, it never completely disappeared. The bourgeoisie would continue to play an important role and make their own claims and demands until the events of Bílá Hora, even if they would never be as successful as they were between 1415 and 1436 (at least in terms of the extent of their rights).

This transformation concerned even the subordinate relations of subjects to their lords (i.e., serfdom), as the feudal social order would not relinquish power easily, and the overall situation in Europe was not ripe for the next advancement.

The Hussite movement strongly loosened the bonds of serfdom for many decades; it was a difficult task for the new Estates' government throughout the fifteenth century and even in the sixteenth century to bring these loosened bonds and relationships back together according to legislative measures (resolutions made by the Diets) and force already in a similar vein to modern police intervention.[49]

Immediately after Sigismund promised in August of 1436 that all the privileges of the nobility and bourgeoisie would be kept, the *Compactata* became the basis of the new state law and continued to function in that manner even after Pope Pius II declared them invalid. Overall, it is undeniable that the Hussite efforts were certainly effective. In order to see the bright contours and understand the specific aspects of their efforts, it is necessary to take a closer look at several key moments which prove that what the Hussites accomplished at Jihlava in 1436 did not fade or perish at all, but progressed even further and with greater intensity.

NOTES

1. See Petr Žatecký, *Deník Petra Žateckého (Liber diurnus)*, trans. František Heřmanský (Prague: Melantrich, 1953), 11–12.

2. See the previous footnote.

3. Šmahel, *Basilejská kompaktáta*, 34.

4. Ibid., 35.

5. Ibid., 36–37.

6. Ibid., 38.

7. Ibid., 41.

8. On the official records, reforms, and politics of the council, see Michiel Decaluwé, Thomas M. Izbicki, and Gerald Christianson, *A Companion to the Council of Basel* (Leiden: Brill, 2016).

9. Šmahel, *Basilejská kompaktáta*, 48.

10. Vaněček, *Dějiny státu a práva v Československu do roku 1945*, 140.

11. See Bartoš, *Husitská revoluce*, 2:175–196.

12. See Martin Lupáč, *Hádání o kompaktátech*, ed. Anna Císařová-Kolářová (Praha: Ústřední církevní nakladatelství, 1953). F.M. Bartoš's epilogue contains much valuable information related to both personalities.

13. Šmahel, *Basilejská kompaktáta*, 56.

14. Ibid., 57. For the original source materials, see Palacký, *Archiv český*, 3:395–464; Palacký, *Urkundliche Beiträge zur Geschichte des Hussitenkrieges*, vol. 2.

15. These respective circumstances are carefully detailed in several historical works. See: Čornej, *Velké dějiny zemí koruny české*, vol. 5; Bartoš, *Husitská revoluce*, 2:143–162; Šmahel, *Basilejská kompaktáta*.

16. Often referred to as Albrecht the Magnanimous.

17. Čornej, *Velké dějiny zemí koruny české*, 5:625.

18. Ibid., 626.

19. Šmahel, *Basilejská kompaktáta*, 59.

20. Čornej, *Velké dějiny zemí koruny české*, 5:627.

21. Ibid., 628.

22. Ibid., 629.

23. Ibid., 630.

24. Ibid.

25. Ibid., 630–631.

26. This town is also commonly known by its Latin name *Alba Regalis*.

27. Šmahel, *Basilejská kompaktáta*, 62.

28. Čornej, *Velké dějiny zemí koruny české*, 5:631.

29. Šmahel, *Basilejská kompaktáta*, 62.

30. Čornej, *Velké dějiny zemí koruny české*, 5:632.

31. Ibid.

32. Ibid., 635.

33. Ibid., 636.

34. Palacký, *Archiv český*, 3:424. Cited from Čornej, *Velké dějiny zemí koruny české*, 5:636.

35. For recent studies on Sigismund, see Wilhelm Baum, *Kaiser Sigismund: Hus, Konstanz und Türkenkriege* (Graz-Wien-Köln: Styria, 1993). The Czech translation is *Císař Sigismund: Kostnice, Hus a války proti Turkům*, trans. Danuše Martinová a Pavel Kocek (Prague: Mladá fronta, 1996). See also František Kavka, *Poslední Lucemburk na českém trůně: králem uprostřed revoluce* (Prague: Mladá fronta, 1998).

36. Bartoš, *Husitská revoluce*, 2:197. Bartoš refers to the edition in Palacký, *Archiv český*, 3:446–449.

37. Ibid.

38. Ibid.

39. The Latin term is *registrum provinciae*. They represent an old source of Bohemian law. In addition to the land registry of real estate owned, the resolutions of diets and the rulings of the Provincial Court were recorded in the Land tables (i.e., seigniorial land registers). See Pavla Burdová, *Desky zemské Království českého* (Praha: Státní ústřední archiv v Praze, 1990).

40. Čornej, *Velké dějiny zemí koruny české*, 5:638.

41. Bartoš, *Husitská revoluce*, 2:198.

42. Čornej, *Velké dějiny zemí koruny české*, 5:639.

43. Vaněček, *Dějiny státu a práva v Československu do roku 1945*, 141.

44. Biographies of both of these protagonists Nicholas of Dresden and Petr Payne are briefly but accurately presented in Kejř, *Husité*, 240–241.

45. Vaněček, *Dějiny státu a práva v Československu do roku 1945*, 141.

46. Ibid.

47. Ibid., 142.

48. Palacký, *Archiv český, 3:419*. Cited from Vaněček, *Dějiny státu a práva v Československu do roku 1945*, 142.

49. Vaněček, *Dějiny státu a práva v Československu do roku 1945*, 142.

Chapter 5

The Constitutional Development of the Bohemian State from 1436 to 1471

The arrival of the emperor (who now enjoyed full rights as king of Bohemia) in Prague marked the beginning of a brief but horror-filled reign which would last for fourteen months. The circumstances surrounding his aggressive re-Catholicization measures are well known and do not need recounting. Of course, everything was done with the full support of the council, and disputes between their theologians and Archbishop Rokycana arose almost immediately. As already mentioned above, several towns did not bow down to Sigismund, while Hradec Králové directly rebelled and was besieged in September of 1436.[1]

Meanwhile, Tábor continued its negotiations with Sigismund and eventually reached a preliminary agreement in November 1436 which led to its promotion as a royal town on January 25, 1437, but also to its subsequent loss of former independence. As it would turn out later, the emperor's victory on this front would prove to be only a temporary one. When part of the kingdom rebelled against his successor, King Albrecht the Magnanimous, Tábor joined the rebellion, and after enduring five weeks of siege efforts still managed to help the Hussites regain control of the land. Kejř evaluated Tábor's situation as follows:

> Its past, teachings, and threat of a possible restoration of its former power was a thorn in everyone's side, both for the Catholics and even for other Utraquists. Forced into a defensive stance, Tábor defended its doctrinal principles at the Utraquist synods which took place between 1441 and 1444, but in the end they were forced to acknowledge Rokycana's position. In 1452, Tábor surrendered to the threat of another siege by regent Jiří of Poděbrady and submitted to the moderate Hussite majority.[2]

As for Hradec Králové, Sigismund conquered it by betrayal and deceit in March of 1437.

The Land Diet which was held in January 1437 is of particular interest from a constitutional standpoint. Responsibility to judge the dispute between the lords and the knights regarding the composition of the Land Court was assigned to Sigismund. The knights desired for their position to be upheld, rightfully considering it as a "conquest" of the revolution. It might be even said that this was the first touchstone to demonstrate just how permanent the new societal and political arrangements truly were. The result was admittedly embarrassing yet significant since the nobility were given twelve seats and the yeomen eight. The office of the chief administrator would be filled by someone from the noble estate. Nevertheless, Sigismund made his political stance quite clear, as only half of the Diet consisted of Hussites while the second half was instead given to Catholics. The "official agenda" of the Diet was to render a decision concerning taxation and on the fate of the lands and property confiscated during the revolution. In the end a high tax was approved, for the gentry vacated the Diet. Thus, the emperor collected the funds necessary to wage war against Hradec Králové, which is the true reason why he needed the tax in the first place.

Sigismund's next steps would prove to be equally unpopular and misguided, such as issuing a special privilege for Kutná Hora that allowed for Catholic and German emigrants to return. He also had his second wife Barbara of Celje (1392–1451) solemnly crowned as the Queen of Bohemia, since in his haste for his own coronation back in 1420, such a ceremony was originally not possible. The coronation ceremony took place in the Saint Vitus Cathedral on February 11, 1437. As was usual with Sigismund, the entire affair was arranged to be as disrespectful to Archbishop Rokycana as possible. After the departure of the Basel legates, ecclesiastical life was to be organized by Bishop Philibert of Coutances, since the council officially deemed Prague's Archbishopric to be vacant; they thus entrusted Philibert to assume leadership of all ecclesiastical matters, despite the fact that he had never been officially appointed as administrator. Rokycana was not taken seriously at all since both his appointment and that of his suffragan bishops were considered non-canonical. Philibert, therefore, acted as de facto administrator and constantly interfered with ecclesiastical arrangements. The Catholic chapter of Prague which only ever granted communion under one kind also returned from its previous exile in Žitava and fully assumed that the administration over the church rightly belonged to them in accordance with canon law. To add insult to injury, Bishop Philibert reconsecrated Saint Vitus Cathedral and called the church life of the Hussites into question, allegedly even going as far as to claim that Prague had only one properly ordained priest—Master Křišťan of Prachatice, who had served at the Church of Saint Michael since 1406.

According to Philibert, all others had gained their positions only during the revolution and not according to the canon law.[3] Afterward, Philibert consecrated new altars and installed relics—essentially centering his efforts on returning church life to its previous state before 1415. Despite the repeated protests of Utraquist inhabitants, members of the banished church orders also started to return to Bohemia. Sigismund worked hand in hand with Philibert in attempting to sway the people to their side (e.g., by installing a shroud with the imprinted image of Jesus Christ into the Chapel of the Holy Cross). Other wondrous exhibition pieces included a cross from Karlštejn, the Bohemian Crown Jewels, and even the plates containing the *Compactata* (not that they actually intended to honor or observe them, however). Čornej commented on the situation as follows:

> The *Compactata* were supposed to fulfill a political role which would help bridge the ideological splitting of the Bohemian nation . . . yet the notion that the *Compactata* would hasten to help overcome the dissenting opinions present within Bohemian ethnic groups proved to be premature. The strong national sentiments of both Calixtine and Catholic parts of the population would slowly blend together only in the second half of the fifteenth century, once the Bohemian Catholics eventually realized that the Compacts of Jihlava were now a permanent part of provincial laws and a guarantee of political stability.[4]

Not every step or action which Sigismund committed, however, should be perceived as being antagonistic or evil. In the spring of 1437, he renewed the privileges of the University of Prague. Although this might initially seem like a purely political move, it granted him no practical benefit in return, since the Council of Basel did not revoke the decrees originally made against the university by the Council of Constance.

Most of his decisions, however, were only made for his own personal interests, such as when he insisted that Jan Rokycana be deposed as administrator by using intrigue and lies. First, Rokycana was stripped of his position as parish priest in the Church of Our Lady before Týn, and the Land Diet deprived him of his rank as administrator. Conservative circles prevailed at the Diet *pro tempore* and they appointed Křišťan of Prachatice as administrator instead. This selection was even approved by Bishop Philibert who was acting in his position as special legate.[5] The rest of the nobility was pacified by the legalization of ownership over all confiscated church property. As a result, Rokycana had to assume a temporary haven in the east of Bohemia, from where he would return in 1448 more than ten years later.

The conquering of Sion Castle became that detonating event which would topple the already fragile order. Jan Roháč of Dubá (d. 1437), a former companion of Jan Žižka (c. 1360–1424), openly trumpeted his hostility against

Sigismund. Sion Castle was ultimately conquered by Hungarian troops, and Jan Roháč was captured and publicly executed alongside his comrades in Prague on September 9, 1437. This was an open insult not only to common Hussites but also to some of the nobles who had willingly cooperated with the emperor in the past. As a result, a number of highly influential conservative Utraquist lords made a stand against Sigismund: Bedřich of Strážnice (d. 1459), Jan Hertvík of Rušinova, Beneš Mokrovous of Hustiřany, and a number of other lords who were mostly from Eastern Bohemia. As a result, Sigismund fled for Hungary, not willing to risk open confrontation.

Queen Barbara joined the Utraquist party (led by Hynce Ptáček of Pirkštejn) against her husband, desiring to become regent of the Crown lands after his death. Ptáček, on the other hand, wanted to prevent the accession Albrecht the Magnanimous and strove for the Jagiellonian dynasty to ascend to the Bohemian throne. Since their plans were not in opposition, they entered into a mutual alliance, with the queen being supported by the Hussites as a result. At the beginning of November 1437, Sigismund hastily fled Prague and headed eastward, with his last official order being the arrest of Queen Barbara. He never reached his destination. He died in Znojmo on December 9, 1437, but his body was buried in Nagyvárad in his beloved Hungary.[6] Another important matter arose immediately after his death—a matter which did not end well at all for the Lands of the Bohemian Crown.

The representatives of towns and nobility had to decide whether or not to accept the emperor's son-in-law Albrecht II of Germany on the throne (in accordance with Sigismund's wishes). This would naturally mean jeopardizing the cause of receiving the chalice during communion, for the royal candidate was a fanatical Catholic without peer. One all-important factor fortunately remained: despite the turbulent times, the Lands of the Bohemian Crown managed to maintain a sense of unity without fracturing and utterly falling apart during the Hussite Wars. Although not everyone became Hussite, the Hussites aspired to religiously convert others and conquer them if need be. The historical concern is exactly how and under what circumstances this actually happened, since the kingdom as a whole managed to persevere. The only exception were the kingdom's fiefdoms of the Bohemian Crown located abroad (*feuda extra curtem*), which were for the most part disbanded.[7]

Several groups played a major role in determining which specific events would happen before a new king could be accepted. The largest of them was undoubtedly the collective union of moderate Hussites and Catholics. Next was the united front of Bohemian nobility, who were seeking to influence the political development of the land and its constitutional order. Next to this union stood the moderate Prague party which included lords from both the lower and the higher nobility, all of whom were passionate Utraquists and influenced to quite some extent by Jan Rokycana. Strongly pro-Hussite towns such as Hradec Králové, Vysoké Mýto, Chrudim, Dvůr Králové, Jaroměř, and others (usually towns in Eastern Bohemia) also belonged to this faction. A rather unique position was enjoyed by the Tábor Union, which managed to preserve its unique character despite all the feasible transformations over the years and the fact that it was now a royal town. The other towns that belonged to this union were Písek, Louny, Klatovy, Žatec, Lanšperk, and Náchod. The Tábor Union was rather problematic for the other factions since it had its own church organization, which did not coincide well with either the constitutional relations of the time or with the newly forming model of society. Čornej appropriately comments on this situation and describes the matter precisely:

> Even the later members of the Táborites did not give up on their view that it was their duty to convince other Hussites (after the *Compactata*) and the universal Church of the importance of strictly adhering to the law of God, which the people of Tábor, according to their own opinion, knew and understood the best of all Christians. After the negotiations with the Council of Basel and the defeat at Lipany, this hope turned into an unrealizable vision (more of an illusion than an ideal), but nevertheless a vision to which Mikuláš of Pelhřimov and his companions continued to remain sympathetic and obstinately faithful. This does not mean that the Táborite party as a whole had lost its sense for reality, as they were willing to engage in politics and purposely change alliances as long as doing so would prolong a state of affairs which was favorable to their own interests. After all, the same applied for the cooperation between Tábor and Ptáček and his allies with the Eastern-Bohemian towns in the case of choosing a possible Polish candidate. Nevertheless, the leaders of Tábor had no doubt realized that not even Jan Rokycana would tolerate the existence of a separate Táborite church organization.[8]

These three factions—conservative, moderate, and Táborite—continued to survive through different transformations until the year 1452. Čornej also comments on the constitutional and legal development and notes that religious and regional matters and concerns of the estates complicated the process leading to the establishment of an Estates-governed state.

Following Sigismund's death, there was a focused attempt to declare the eleven-year-old Polish Prince Kazimír as the new ruler of Bohemia. Albrecht II of Germany ultimately assumed the throne in circumstances which were not very distinguished. Considering all the forces directed at preventing precisely such a scenario, a closer investigation is required.

First, the union of moderates and Catholics was more powerful than the other two parties. After Albrecht II promised to reintegrate the Margraviate of Moravia under the Bohemian Crown (the question of whether the Bohemian

throne was hereditary or a matter of election being a major point of conten-
tion), the House of Habsburg was accepted on the throne despite any opposition. As records tell us, the representatives of the Estates chose and selected
him and acknowledged the hereditary claims of Elizabeth of Luxembourg
(1409–1442) and the older dynastic treaties. It seemed as if the attempt at the
Estates monarchy had failed and that everything was returning to its former
status. However, it would be a grave mistake to assume as much, since in
this case there was no true election or choice of which to speak, because the
candidate proved his claim by being the husband of his heir.

Albrecht II of Germany arrived in Prague on June 13, 1438, much to the
displeasure of the majority of the people, who did not want him to be coro-
nated. The coronation ritual, arranged according to Charles IV, was not and
could not be fully observed; the ceremony was not attended by the archbishop
of Prague, for there was no bishop! Bishop Pavel of Miličín, who was called
to Prague, could not perform the ritual according to the original order, because
an important part of the ceremony (anointing the head of the new king and
placing the diadem upon his head) depended on the presence of an archbishop. The entire coronation is described by Čornej.[9] Bishop Pavel of Miličín
anointed the king on his head, shoulders, and chest, but the literary sources
do not include who was responsible for handling the coronation insignia. The
royal crown was bestowed on the head of the king by four members of high
nobility together with Bishop Pavel. This was quite a radical departure from
how the process was performed in neighboring countries, since it was always
the task of a metropolitan to crown the king. Considering the vast importance
that the coronation ritual possessed, this particular event was a downright
revolutionary step; the participation of high nobility in the act of crowning
made it adamantly clear by whose will a person would become king.

King Albrecht was born as the son of Albrecht IV and Johanna Sophia of
Bavaria in 1397.[10] Following the death of his father in 1404, his guardian
became Sigismund of Luxembourg. In 1420, he fought alongside Oldřich of
Rožmberk against Tábor, and in 1423 he married Sigismund's only daughter
and was given the Margraviate of Moravia as a fief on that special occasion. As a result, when the moderate Hussite wing attempted and ultimately
failed to promote the Polish candidacy, Moravia maintained a significant
importance.

While the coronation of Albrecht II made it seem as if the Bohemian
throne were safely secured for the Habsburg line for a long time, time would
quickly prove otherwise. In 1439, the king marched against the Turkish
invasion of Hungary. Even though he survived the actual battles, he became
ill with dysentery; this disease would claim his life on October 27, 1439,
in Neszmély near Komárno. Shortly after his death on February 22, 1440,
Queen Elizabeth gave birth to a son in Komárno who was given the name

Ladislaus Posthumous (1440–1457).[11] The queen fought fiercely to secure hereditary rights for her son, and as a result he became the king of Hungary in 1444, although the actual government in the Kingdom of Hungary was exercised for him by regent-governor János Hunyadi (1406–1456). This period of interregnum would prove to be beneficial to Bohemia, as in the absence of the king it once again fell to the Land Diets to govern the kingdom. The Land Diet was loathe to accept Ladislaus and his hereditary rights and instead opted to elect Albrecht III, Duke of Bavaria (1401–1460) as new monarch in June 1440.[12] This decision proved to be quite disastrous when the man in question met with Bohemian representatives at the end of August in Cham; he disappointed the delegates of the Bohemian Diet by choosing not to accept the crown. His primary reason for refusing was most likely his fear of the Habsburgs, the council, and the pope. The state of royal property in Bohemia was also in very poor condition, and the Bohemian lords demanded for Bavaria to be annexed to the Bohemian Crown. It soon became obvious that the Bohemians would not have a king on the throne anytime soon. After thirteen long years, the time was dawning when the preservation of the estate privileges and benefits were at stake.

Before the actual election in the summer of the same year, the moderate Hussites led by Hynce Ptáček of Pirkštejn created a union of East-Bohemian regions, which was joined by the region of Boleslav under the leadership of none other than Lord Jiří of Poděbrady. This created the foundation for the future Estates Utraquist power in Bohemia, which would play an increasingly important role in society after the eventual election of Jiří of Poděbrad to the throne in 1458 and would become the central power.[13]

Between 1441 and 1442 there were negotiations concerning the occupation of the Bohemian throne with the rulers of other countries, but they were literally to no avail. The religious meetings at the time indicate that the Hussite movement was hardly restricted to the high nobility whose singular interest would only be ratifying the *Compactata*. In 1441, Jan Rokycana was already accepted as the administrator of the Utraquist priesthood in Eastern-Bohemian regions, and the Synod in Kutná Hora (which took place in October of the same year) recognized him as the head of the entire Utraquist Church.

This was supported at the Land Diet in January 1444, which also tackled several doctrinal issues of the church, ultimately defending Rokycana's teachings. One of the most influential figures of the Bohemian Diet was Hynce Ptáček of Pirkštejn. Born in 1400, he participated at the Battle of Lipany on the victorious side. When state offices were restored in 1437, he became the highest court-master (*Hofmeister*)[14] and provincial judge. During the critical years after the deaths of Sigismund and Albrecht II, he was elected as an East-Bohemian hetman in 1440 and became an informal leader of the Utraquists. He died on August 27, 1440, at a relatively young age. Jiří of Poděbrady assumed leadership of the East-Bohemian *Landfriede*, and his role would prove to be absolutely crucial—much greater than merely as a replacement or substitute leader. Jiří descended from the family of lords of Kunštát and was the son of the Hussite commander Viktorín of Kunštát (1403–1427).[15] His role in the legal and constitutional history of the Bohemian kingdom bears a great importance for understanding Hussite movement in general. Fortunately, it was relatively straightforward and not all that difficult to follow. After he assumed leadership among the Hussites when Ptáček passed away, he maintained it for the rest of his life. He quickly proved himself a decisive leader fully devoted to the restoration of the kingdom. During the dangerous episode when the Catholic nobility were taking aggressive measures and readying to march against Utraquism, Jiří did not hesitate and responded by immediately seeking to occupy Prague in 1448. Another instance was the conquering of Tábor. As already mentioned, despite being a royal town, Tábor still retained considerable influence (even if more from an ideological standpoint than from a position of power). Jiří, apparently supported by Rokycana, was aware of this and laid siege to the town in early September 1452. Since then, Tábor was effectively excluded from the political life of the land completely. Jiří was an energetic nobleman who, in his attempts to restore the kingdom, proclaimed himself as the regent-governor because he considered that achieving the recognition of Ladislaus Posthumous as King of Bohemia was the only proper means of stabilizing the country. He proved successful in his endeavor: Ladislaus was indeed crowned king of Bohemia on October 28, 1453. The Land Diet itself confirmed Jiří as governor by electing him in April of 1452, although he had already held the office without an election. Because Ladislaus was still under-age at the time, Jiří retained his executive power and continued striving to maintain a balance between the Catholic and Hussite nobility. Jiří was also responsible for a partial restoration of royal estates and property. In terms of dealing with opposition and his enemies, Jiří eliminated all dissenters without inhibition. When dealing with the radicals, he favored military force, though the more wealthy and influential ones were given offices instead. When Ladislaus suddenly died in 1457, there was an urgent need to address the ensuing crisis regarding succession. Perhaps unsurprisingly, Jiří was at one time falsely accused of poisoning the king, although a modern pathological examination of the king's remains revealed the true cause of his death to be leukemia, absolving Jiří of any lingering suspicions.[16]

The entire process of the constitutional development of the Bohemian state still needed to mature in order to reach its climactic turning point: without the occurrence of such a breaking point, such development would not have been ensured, and the whole Hussite Revolution would prove to have been in vain. The election of Jiří as king guaranteed that there would be no turning back, neither at this point nor ever after. Many other candidates were considered at first: Emperor Frederick III, Holy Roman Emperor (1415–1493), Polish Casimir IV Jagiellon (1427–1492), and even William III, Landgrave of Thuringia (1425–1482). But it soon became obvious that no Catholic ruler would be willing to promise to uphold the *Compactata*. That is why the nobility had to take a radical step and elect their own Hussite king. It was a difficult decision to make, even when the Catholic nobility was convinced (whether by coercion or bribery) to support the election. His election took place on March 2, 1458, at the Old Town Hall. Representatives of neighboring Lands of the Bohemian Crown were not in attendance, as they were Catholic and resolutely opposed to the election. The Moravian Catholic nobility also did not agree with the process and did not vote for him. As a Hussite and as King of Bohemia, Jiří was a diligent defender of the Basel Compacts, even though both of his wives—Kunhuta of Šternberk (1425–1449) and then Johana of Rožmitál (c. 1430–1474)—only received communion under one kind.

He also behaved skillfully toward the papal legates. On the eve of his coronation he promised them his obedience to the pope as well as the persecution of heretics. The papal legates interpreted his promise as waiving the right of receiving the chalice, but that was a grave misunderstanding; and concerning the persecution of heretics, King Jiří understood the word heretics not as a reference to Hussites but rather the members of the emerging Unity of Brethren, against whom the king did indeed pursue persecution as he previously promised he would. Although Jiří was not religiously intolerant, he saw the Unity of the Brethren as a political successor to Tábor and its radicalism. His opinion, however, did not correspond to the truth, as the Unity of the Brethren movement was itself far removed from radicalism.

The reception of Jiří in the near future did not bode well for several countries. Shortly after his election, Jiří had to engage in military intervention against Albrecht VI, Archduke of Austria (1418–1463), who did not want to surrender his claim over Moravia. Silesia and both Upper and Lower Lusatia accepted Jiří as their king some time between 1459 and 1460. Throughout his rule, Jiří proved himself a very skilful ruler, capable in both diplomacy and warfare. He also managed to reach an agreement with Emperor Frederick III in 1459 in which he was confirmed to receive the Crown lands of Bohemia as a fief, and was probably also confirmed in the rank of prince-elector with all of its privileges of the Kingdom of Bohemia guaranteed. He subsequently provided military support for the emperor on multiple occasions.

Otherwise, perhaps the greatest challenge to Jiří's rule was that some of his local dissenters perceived him as a heretic and a person of low social class at birth, who in their eyes had usurped the throne without having any true right to assume it. Even until the end of his rule, Jiří never managed to completely refute these objections. Yet, as a stalwart Hussite and defender of receiving the chalice, he did everything in his power to uphold and defend the *Compactata* even against serious opposition.

The king requested for Pope Pius II to confirm the Basel Compacts (since they were only ever agreed upon with the council and not with the pope himself) and also tried to have Jan Rokycana officially ordained as archbishop of Prague. The pope unfortunately denied both, stating that the chalice was permitted only in a specific situation (with certain conditions) and that the Roman Curia had never agreed to the *Compactata* in the first place (which was technically true). As the next series of events would show, the Catholic Church never actually intended to honor its promises or to uphold the agreements with any degree of seriousness. Pius II went so far as to summon the king before the ecclesiastical court, and his successor Paul II did the same only a year later.[17]

In 1466, the pope officially placed Jiří under an interdict, formally divested him of his throne and property (despite having no right to do either), and declared a crusade against him. This is only more proof that the Roman Church had never actually changed its position and had intended all along to exterminate the Hussites through persistent efforts.

However, history repeated itself once again and the crusade failed, though for a somewhat different reason than previous attempts at reconquest. Jiří's son-in-law, the Hungarian King Matthias Corvinus (1443–1490), led the quests. The following events are well known: at the Battle of Vilémov, Jiří captured the king and released him only when the prisoner swore upon the condition that he would no longer wage war against Bohemia. Unfortunately, Corvinus violated his oath at the first opportunity available and allowed himself to be elected as King of Bohemia by the Catholic Estates in Olomouc on May 3, 1469. This action certainly created a perilous situation for Jiří since this choice was acknowledged by many Moravian lords and the representatives of the neighboring Lands of the Bohemian Crown (especially Silesia and Lusatia). In fact, Jiří remained the king only within Hussite Bohemia, while his rule in the other Lands of the Bohemian Crown was only formal. Even worse, there was the ever-increasing threat of invasion from the Turks, which prompted Jiří to attempt to create an organization of European rulers who would counter the threat in 1462. Because this organization did not include the pope, these efforts were ultimately unable to be realized.

The aim of this work is not to evaluate and judge Jiří's governance from a historical perspective; many notable historians have already done so. Nevertheless, one should remember the importance which his reign had for the further constitutional development of the Bohemian state. Jiří knew all too well that he would not have been successful in establishing his own dynasty, even as preferable as that might have been as an ideal. Not only did his descendants lack his proficient leadership skills, but the rulers of surrounding countries would never accept their rule either. He, therefore, reached an agreement that after his death he would not be succeeded by his own sons but by the Polish royal Jagiellonian dynasty. Jiří did not live long enough to be very disappointed when (following his death) his own sons gradually moved away from receiving the chalice.

The Jagiellonians promised during secret negotiations that they would be sufficiently tolerant toward the chalice and would respect the political constraints arranged by the substantial power of the Bohemian Estates (i.e., the Bohemian Land Diet). King Jiří was afraid that after his departure from this world the kingdom would once again be thrown into turmoil, which could very well jeopardize the Hussite legacy. His struggle for the *Compactata*—and by extension the legal form of the Bohemian state—was viewed thus by legal historian Jiří Kejř:

> Every section of Bohemian society was interested in the new religious fabric and arrangement. The Compacts—an agreement between the Church Council and Bohemia—was the very first instance in recorded history of the Catholic Church making concessions in both liturgy and doctrine. Bohemia was permitted to have two recognized co-existing faiths; in addition to the universal Church, Utraquism lived there with its own separate church organization and administration. Of course, the fact that the territory of a prominent state had two separate ecclesiastical constituents in it (i.e., "two kinds of people") living in it, naturally meant that there would be permanent tension and strife. When Pope Pius II dismissed the Compacts as being invalid in 1462, the Utraquist part of the population refused the decision and instead the Land Diet declared them as binding and obligatory for the Bohemian state, forever confirming and cementing their constitutional character. Maintaining a useful balance between the two religious elements was one of the primary objectives of King Jiří´s political balance sheet.[18]

After King Jiří died on March 22, 1471, the Land Diet assembled together almost immediately on May 20 in Kutná Hora. Their haste was well-placed, for King Corvinus was doing everything within his power to claim the throne for himself by force. The Bohemian Estates acted swiftly because time was of the essence, and they sought to solve this pressing matter quickly at all costs. As the primary decision-making body in the land (a privilege that would last for a long time), they were afraid that unless they pursued a decisive course of action, then someone else (i.e., some military force) would determine the heritage of the Bohemian Crown. Delegates of the Polish king addressed the Diet with Dobiesław Kurozwęcki as their official spokesperson, and if the records are reliable he made a great impression on the gathered Estates. Johann Beckenschlager (c. 1435–1489), Bishop of Eger, who represented Matthias

Corvinus, aimed at nothing less than to garner sympathy for Matthias and weaken the negotiations of the Diet by fracturing their unity. This proved unsuccessful, however, and the Hungarian delegation departed on May 25, 1471. A consensus was reached only two days later, and the Jagiellonian dynasty was elected to the Bohemian throne—much to the angry dismay of Corvinus, who in Jihlava pronounced himself as the ruler of Bohemia. This exploit was a futile one, as Pope Paul II (1417–1471) did not validate his claim legally and left him without confirmation as the King of Bohemia.

The official delegation of the Bohemian Estates then traveled to Kraków where the election of Vladislaus II of Hungary (1456–1516) to the Bohemian throne was finalized between June 15–16. Vladislaus accepted his election, promised to uphold the *Compactata* (his most important promise), and pledged to negotiate with the pope in order to gain papal recognition for Bohemia and Moravia. This papal recognition was certainly necessary, because the *Compactata* would never have been accepted otherwise. He also committed to

to uphold the Land privileges and the Estates' concessions, to not allow land, town, or spiritual offices to be occupied by foreigners, to not entrust Karlštejn Castle and the Crown Jewels contained therein to anyone without prior consent from the Estates community, to protect the rights and dowry of Queen Johana (now a widow), and finally, to not harm any of Jiří's sons and to settle their debts.[19]

When word reached the pope about the agreement, he was furious and railed that Vladislaus had been elected by a band of heretics, which meant that his election was null and void. Corvinus's engaging diplomatic maneuver was simply to oppose the election by offering absurd conditions as the basis upon which he would be willing to tolerate the Jagiellonian election. For example, he proposed a simultaneous coronation of two kings of Bohemia, which of course the Poles refused to accept.

The struggle to find a suitable successor for Jiří ended in victory for the Jagiellonians. In August 1471, Vladislaus finally entered Prague to attend his coronation. The constitutional act of his coronation has been accurately described as follows:

On Thursday, August 27, the coronation occurred in the Saint Vitus Cathedral. The partially faded tiara and golden apple were hastily gilded again in order to give the ceremony its proper radiance, which was observed not only by the guests from German the lands but also members of the king's Polish entourage—which included such persons as Dobiesław Kurozwęcki, Stanisław Ostroróg, Paweł Jasieński, and the king's own tutor and famous chronicler Jan

Długosz (1415–1480), who was offered but declined the office of Archbishop of Prague. The more observant spectators were careful to notice that the coronation itself was performed by Mikuláš Próchnicki, Bishop of Kamianets-Podilskyi with the assistance of the Bishop of Chełm, Wincenty Kiełbasa (c. 1425–1479), and suffragan Bishop Paweł from Kraków, none of whom held prominent positions within the Polish episcopate. The very fact that the crown of Saint Václav rested upon the head of young Vladislaus and not Corvinus was a major victory for Polish diplomacy. It was also the culmination of the Jagiellonian dynasty's long-standing aspiration for the Bohemian throne and of the long-term party line of Hussite politics which had already been considering a Polish ruler since 1420.[20]

Only at this moment in history was the Hussite struggle for a new Estates fulfilled. Only at this point did all of the changes and developments that had taken place from 1420 onward become secured and irreversible—even if perhaps not exactly in the way that individual Hussites parties would have wished for them to be in the past. And although the ruler received under only one kind, he swore to uphold the essence of the Hussite movement which was first formulated in the *Four Articles,* then reaffirmed and specified later within the *Compactata.* The manner in which Vladislaus's reign was enacted was not as important as the fact that the Kingdom of Bohemia was no longer automatically governed in a dynastic fashion; additionally, the Bohemian Estates played a decisive role in the election and reception of the king as well as in the political life of the land due to a major shift in the social composition and status of political and constitutionally legal freedoms.

The situation in Moravia developed in a slightly different way than in Bohemia, but in general achieved a similar status. As the Catholic clergy in Moravia retained a strong position, it never became a truly Hussite region. Their presence was not enough, however, to completely halt the spread of the principle of estates, which had strongly developed and would come to play a major role in the region years later. The legal development of Moravia is an interesting topic for further research; it was usually governed by the leading members of the ruling dynasty. Only later was the position of margrave always a Bohemian king, who usually had his special representative in Moravia—a provincial hetman (*capitaneus terrae*). Despite all of these observed differences, the estates also developed in Moravia (though the Catholic clergy were not excluded from the Estates' compartmentalization as was the case in Bohemia).

Overall, the Hussite movement left a permanent mark on Bohemia and contributed to the fact that its constitutional development moved forward in the specific direction indicated above. Kejř noted that "neighboring lands of the Bohemian Crown remained virtually untouched by the Hussite movement, while from the outset the Duchies of Silesia and the Lusatian forces were definitely categorized among the opponents of the Hussite Revolution and fought against it throughout the wars, sometimes with even more cruelty than any other hostile power."[21] Some of Silesia's duchies were governed by a local duke or by a hetman, whereas both sides of Lusatia were governed by special officials called *fojt*.[22] Therefore, these lands remained untouched by the revolution and only later experienced a measure of change, although the effects were associated with a different power than the Estates. Although towns would come to play a much greater role there as well, that is another chapter which is unconnected to the Hussite struggle.

In recent years, the Hussite movement has increasingly been questioned in many respects, undoubtedly due in large part to the ways in which it was arbitrarily interpreted and willfully misinterpreted during the Communist regime by a Marxist philosophy of history. Hussitism, however, simply cannot be denied as a religious reform movement and as a principle. One only need remember Palacký's thesis: whenever the Kingdom of Bohemia raised its sword during the Hussite period, it was not solely for material gain but predominantly for defending the freedom of the human spirit. This is a valid understanding regarding both religion and law, for the Bohemian Estates which united and rose up against foreign intervention were indeed not only fighting to uphold their own freedom, but also the freedom of the whole state. The fact that it resulted in a major constitutional movement and in the transformation of their function within the state can be seen as a natural conclusion of such principles and events.

AN EXCURSION INSTEAD OF AN EPILOGUE

This overview of the legal development of the Hussite state, which rightfully concluded with reference to the ascension of Vladislaus II of Hungary to the Bohemian throne in 1471, would not be complete without recalling an important legal measure mentioned at the beginning of this study. The *Religious Peace of Kutná Hora* (1485) had long been in preparation and was a natural consequence of all of the previously existing legal developments. At the same time, however, it was an unprecedented agreement with absolutely no equivalent before the European Reformation.

The coexistence of Catholics and Utraquists in the kingdom was never an easy affair. As an example, one only need refer to the rebellion of 1483 when Prague and its allied towns rose up against the king. This uprising, during which the Utraquist insurgents seized both Vyšehrad and Prague Castle, initially appeared threatening. In retrospect, it is hardly that surprising at all, since the Utraquist party was continuously oppressed and unable to reach any agreement of a decent modus vivendi with the Catholics even after many years. The king, already furious from the fact that the Utraquist Union accepted Prague as a member at the end of 1483, interpreted the event as a personal affront to his own dignity.[23] In October 1483, the representatives of the three Prague towns made an agreement concerning cooperative action toward the various problems at hand, with all of the town burghers gradually joining the agreement as well. The treaty is a rare document which reveals the state of confessional circumstances at the time. The agreement promised to maintain loyalty to King Vladislaus, but only if he were to uphold everything which he had promised during his coronation. This stance would seem perfectly logical in itself, but there were also several other requirements not originally included in the *Compactata*. For example, communion under both kinds was also to be served to children, and church worship services were to be held in the Czech language. They also protested against the prohibition of mixed marriages between Hussites and Catholics and against the notion that the Calixtine Church was not officially recognized as part of the universal church. In the future, communion would be served exclusively under both kinds in Prague, while receiving under one kind was to be forbidden. The Utraquist character of the University of Prague was to be preserved and canons, Catholic priests, and all Catholics were to be expelled. The particular wording employed in the document was reminiscent of the radical step taken in 1420. The University of Prague officially espoused the document in 1484, going as far as to confirm their agreement in the University Registry in April 1484. The current situation (whose prospects were already doubtful) started to unravel with the death of Jan Tovačovský of Cimburk in November 1483; in him the Utraquist Union lost a prominent representative and others were seeking to compromise.

The king eventually reached an agreement with the Prague towns in September 1484. Prague upheld all of its essential demands, but in exchange they had to return any property confiscated from the church and from the Jews; in addition, both Vyšehrad and Prague Castle had to be returned to the ruler. The king appointed town councilors according to the wishes of the Prague towns. Most importantly, this agreement would become the prerequisite for future negotiations regarding religious peace in the land. Although such discussions had already taken place between 1481 and 1483, the uprising of the Prague towns resulted in a failure to reach an agreement. Nevertheless, the roadblocks were removed, and the pathway was now open for a new session of debates, with the foreseen expectation being that the peace would last for thirty-two years. Further preparation and refinement of the treaty was permitted until the moment of its presentation in its final form at the Land Diet in Kutná Hora, March 13–20, 1485. The treaty itself became known as the *Religious Peace of Kutná Hora*. Its most important element was the stipulation that both members of the Estates community and serfs should possess freedom of religion. Therefore, they could receive communion either under both kinds or only one kind, and none would be allowed to pressure others to change their confession.

> The problem with receiving the holy communion was defined precisely by this resolution. Since the priests were obliged to give the Eucharist to "the common folk in accordance with the tradition of their parish and forbidden to pressure anyone towards one or the other kind in both secret or public," believers had the right to attend churches with parishioners of their actual confession. The document also stipulated that all existing parishes must remain in their existing confession.[24]

The agreement was expected to be valid for thirty-one years, since everyone expected complicated debates with the pope on the matter to take a certain amount of time, after which the contract would be renewed indefinitely. The importance of the *Compactata* as well as of the specific freedoms which Sigismund promised the Hussites were highly accentuated. The treaties made between the emperor and Prague (and other towns) were not mentioned, since the recent treaty concluded between Vladislaus and the Union effectively achieved the same result: Prague had the exclusive right to serve only under both kinds. There was only one detail which prevented the agreement from addressing all problems at once: it did not apply to the Unity of the Brethren, since the movement was considered heretical and could be persecuted. Later in the sixteenth century some members of the nobility joined the movement; it thus became legally tolerable. A proper solution would finally arise in 1609 with the *Letter of Majesty* issued by Rudolf II (1552–1612). Until that time the Unity of the Brethren was considered to be a sect and thus had to endure without any legal protection whatsoever. This could be seen as the sole flaw or weak point of the *Religious Peace of Kutná Hora*. Nevertheless, the mere existence of this epoch-making treaty meant that people understood the futility of further religious conflict. The protagonists of our drama

> guaranteed freedom of religion to members of both confessions in accordance with the Compacts, which extended even to the serfs. On a *practical level*, they embarked upon continuing the principles undergirding the Hussite Revolution and gradually adopted those same principles on a *theoretical level*. The *Religious Peace of Kutná Hora* organically grew from the bedrock of the revolutionary reality, and at the same time foreshadowed certain principles of the Bohemian Confession of 1575 (*Confessio Bohemica*). It was fundamentally different from the solution birthed by the *Peace of Augsburg* (1555) in the German domains of the Holy Roman Empire, which was based on the principle

of *cuius regio, eius religio* ('whose realm, his religion'). By comparison, serfs in the Kingdom of Bohemia had no obligation to belong to the same confession as their authorities, but the consequences of this principle (anticipatory of European development by a century) were able to cause certain difficulties and unrest in the economic sphere.[25]

The fact that this treaty was actually concluded was undoubtedly due to the search for a common good to which even the divine law would be subservient. Indeed, according to a radical Hussite interpretation, the law of God would never condone receiving communion under only one kind without being abdicated in the name of the common good (*bonum commune*). Nonetheless, the truth remains that this level of religious tolerance concerning the question of confession was reached by people who had already experienced the cruelty of war. Those experiences contributed to the particular way in which they pursued agreement, since their approach was not only sufficiently pragmatic but also quite groundbreaking in terms of overcoming medieval rigidness and confessional limitations.

Due to the newly established validity of peace, there was a significant increase in mixed marriages among members of the high nobility. Although historians agree that the principle of non-confessional Christianity (as evidenced within the circles of high nobility) was not yet fully integrated among all social classes at that time, the nobility intermingled on the basis of the Estates and the principle of confessionalism slowly ceased to apply. This was especially true for the highest members of society, since noblemen had closer relationships with each other through the Estates without church interference. For the various towns (and especially for Utraquist Prague), this posed a completely new danger to be borne in mind, as they had to remain vigilant in their defense of Utraquism at all costs. Therefore, Prague

pushed for a fundamental exception in the resolution of the Diet. There was simply no other way to accomplish it, for along with the whole town estate, it owed its newfound political status to the Hussite Revolution, which uplifted towns as a political power within the Land Diet. Their premonition that members of the high nobility would strengthen the Estates' communality and try to undermine the town's status and influence after the confessional barrier between them was dissolved proved to be well-justified, as such efforts could be observed happening even before the religious peace was fully implemented. Already in 1484, a demand was put forward by the royal council for the royal towns to surrender the privilege which granted them the third vote and thus representation at the Diet.[26]

Of course, no such privilege existed, since it was the result of a long legal process and not an "honor" which could be taken away so easily. Although the nobility did not expressly want to deny the rights of the towns for representation in this particular case, they did demand that those rights should be duly justified. On the other hand, at the Diet of Kutná Hora in 1485, the lords and knights also claimed outright that the estate of towns was less free (i.e., had fewer rights) than the nobility, since they belonged to the royal chamber. This conflict would prove to be long-lasting and quite critical even much later, though not directly in the Lands of the Bohemian Crown, primarily because societal development was forcefully halted in 1620—by the kingdom itself! After all, the discrepancies between the nobility and the bourgeoisie would prove to be the essence of the early modern revolutions in the Netherlands and in England.

Legal historian Kejř did not consider the religious peace established at Kutná Hora as a predecessor to the later-established "freedom of religion" as the concept is understood today; he argued that it simply was not yet possible at the time, using the fate of the Unity of the Brethren as an evident example. Yet even he could not deny that the

> Bohemian efforts at settling religious disputes, despite all of the setbacks, misunderstandings, and often animosity, eventually led to the *Religious Peace of Kutná Hora* in 1485, achieving a result which far outshone the rest of contemporary Europe and unveiled the path toward resolving religious conflicts in the future. Even in this the Hussite movement ultimately manifested its importance and viability.[27]

The Diet at Kutná Hora also adopted other resolutions which enabled the normalization of life in the land again. One of those concerned a rather complicated issue, namely the Provincial Court (*iudicium terre*) which had not been in session for a number of years (partly due to the inability of representatives from the lower and higher nobility to agree on their proportional representation). The proportion of representatives retained the original number (12:8), the arrangement of seats, the manner of reporting findings, and the variance concerning land records. As a result, the Provincial Court finally resumed its function in June 1485—after almost twenty years of inaction. Everything was successful, so the king officially confirmed the measures regarding the Provincial Court in the spring of 1487. Čornej explains that

> the disputes between the higher and lower nobility concerning the provincial court somewhat prevented the political offensive of the nobles against the royal towns, but ultimately did not change the unmitigated historical importance of the Diet at Kutná Hora, which ended the Hussite period in March 1485 by declaring religious peace between the Utraquists and Catholics and also cleared

the way for the establishment of a new type of state—one governed by the Estates and not just the nobility alone.[28]

The historical chain of events which led to the declaration of religious peace has been closely analyzed and chronologically detailed by Ferdinand Hrejsa (1867–1953). Surprisingly, however, even he did not make a formal judgment and ascribe to those events their true level of importance, apparently due to the deep impression of having to describe the difficulty period of the Unity of the Brethren. Hrejsa also avoided making any greater evaluations or conclusions, and despite his extensive work on the subject, the long-term legal consequences of these events seem to be lacking.

NOTES

1. See Jan Blahoslav Lášek, "Kněz Ambrož a východočeské husitství, Hradec a Oreb" in *Theologická revue* 70 (1999): 45–57. The English version appears as Jan B. Lášek, "Priest Ambrož and East-Bohemian Utraquism: Hradec and Oreb," in *The Bohemian Reformation and Religious Practice*, vol. 3, eds. Zdeněk V. David and David R. Holeton (Prague: Academy of Sciences of the Czech Republic, 2000), 105–118.

2. Kejř, *Husité*, 193.

3. Čornej, *Velké dějiny zemí koruny české*, 5:646.

4. Ibid., 648.

5. See Jakub Malý, *Vlastenecký slovník historický* (Prague: Rohlíček a Sievers, 1877), 123–124.

6. This is modern day Oradea in Romania.

7. For more details, see Čornej, *Velké dějiny zemí koruny české*, 5:654.

8. Čornej and Bártlová, *Velké dějiny zemí koruny české*, 6:49.

9. Ibid., 51.

10. Though outdated, see Friedrich Kurz, *Österreich unter K. Albrecht dem Zweyten* (Vienna: Kupffer und Singer, 1835); see also Pavla Vošahlíková et al., *Bibliografický slovník českých zemí*, 1. Sešit A (Prague: Libri, 2004), 55–56.

11. Jaroslav Čechura, *České země v letech 1437–1526: Mezi Sigismundem a Jiřím z Poděbrad (1437–1471)*, vol. 1 (Prague: Libri, 2010); see also Petr Čornej, "Ladislav Pohrbek," in Marie Ryantová and Petr Vorel, eds., *Čeští králové* (Prague: Paseka, 2008), 251–261.

12. He is also known as Albrecht III the Pious of Bavaria-Munich.

13. Rudolf Urbánek, *České dějiny: Věk poděbradský*, vol. 3/1–4 (Prague: Jan Laichter, 1915–1962); see also Otakar Odložilík, *The Hussite King: Bohemia in European Affairs 1440–1471* (New Brunswick: Rutgers University Press, 1965).

14. The Latin term is *supremus magister curiae*.

15. For the most relevant literature on his life, see Frederick Gotthold Heymann, *George of Bohemia, King of Heretics* (Princeton: Princeton University Press, 1965); see also Odložilík, *The Hussite King*.

16. Čornej and Bártlová, *Velké dějiny zemí koruny české*, 6:128–129.

17. Ibid., 200ff. Although the struggle between Jiří and the papacy has already been described many times, the most recent research from Čornej will be used here for the purposes of this study.

18. Kejř, *Husité*, 193.

19. Čornej and Bártlová, *Velké dějiny zemí koruny české*, 6:408.

20. Ibid., 6:409.

21. Kejř, *Husité*, 194.

22. *Vogt* in German; *advocatus* in Latin.

23. For a comprehensive overview of these historical events, see Ferdinand Hrejsa, *Dějiny křesťanství v Československu: Za krále Vladislava a Ludvíka. Před světovou reformací a za reformace* (Prague: Husova československá evangelická fakulta bohoslovecká, 1948), 4:41–60; see also Čornej and Bártlová, *Velké dějiny zemí koruny české*, 6:452–457.

24. Ibid., 6:454.

25. Ibid., 6:456.

26. Ibid.

27. Kejř, *Husité*, 194.

28. Čornej and Bártlová, *Velké dějiny zemí koruny české*, 6:457.

Conclusion

Throughout this study, several aspects of the meaning, importance, and influence of the Hussite period for the overall transformation of both society and the state as an institution have been presented. The constitutional relations created between 1419 and 1471 could have never arisen if it were not for the appearance of Master Jan Hus, and especially all of the later figures who formulated the *Four Articles of Prague* and defended them, weapon in hand. A major role in the transformation of the state was played by two political forces which originally opposed one another, then stood together side by side against a common threat, and eventually even struggled together against the king: the Estates and the towns.

When the power of the monarch began wavering due to various reasons (e.g., weakness, inconsistencies, conflicts over succession after a ruler's death, etc.), the balance of power shifted in favor of the nobility, who slowly started organizing themselves as estates. The first basic indicators of this shift could already be observed during the feeble reign of Václav IV. Depending on the specific location, similar developments would occur sooner or later in other European countries also.[1]

Vaněček claimed that the class struggle prompted the emergence and development of the Estates by arguing that those who had power needed to unify against the peasant wars. But this would be a major misinterpretation, as class struggle barely existed at all in the Hussite movement; rather, there was an ideological kinship with "peasants." They all agreed on the *Four Articles,* and their unity lasted for quite a significant period. However, the mutual and constant rivalry between the nobility and distrust between the individual estates (especially between nobility and clergy, though also between nobility and towns) did play a visible role in the Hussite movement.

The Estates which arose during the late Middle Ages were effectively a new form of organization which could be observed in the Lands of the Bohemian Crown since the early fifteenth century. As a major landowner and de facto feudal power in its own right, the church would soon begin dwindling due to the radical appearance of the Hussites, with three different estates arising in its place instead. These estates would continue to engage in mutual dialogue and constant power struggle while sharing the same deeply held religious values. These estates were the lords, the knights, and the towns. The serfs did not originally belong to this new hierarchical scheme, though there was a "peasant estate" of sorts. At the height of the Hussite Revolution there was a notable loosening of such feudal relations, so even the peasants had their unique and irreplaceable role to play. Soon, however, the three estates understood that such an arrangement could not last forever and that the peasants had to return to their original feudal station, or else the whole fabric of society would collapse. The Estates in Hussite and post-Hussite Bohemia would then realize and implement their true power in the Land Diets, where they decided not only upon laws but also upon who would sit on the throne.

> One of the unmistakable characteristics of the emerging Estates was that in the Hussite Revolution the town delegates commonly participated in the Diets alongside the nobility, while the lower nobility were definitely separated from the higher nobility even at that time. For example, one can observe from 1437 that the representatives seated at the Diets were composed of knights and lords in a certain numerical proportion; then with the proviso of the Land Constitution from 1549 and its enactment establishing the estates in Bohemia as being definitely three in number (i.e., the lords, the knights, and the towns), it was a clear sign that the societal and political development of the Estates was accomplished.[2]

Each of the three estates would eventually have its own specific order, but this only occurred after the Hussite period had already expired.

The Diets, and especially the Land Diets (which were the absolutely decisive political force during the Hussite period), consisted of representatives from the estates; the same estates which had recently showed their countenance by struggling among themselves (and the monarch) for power in the state were now electing who would have the right to ascend to the Bohemian throne. There was no force majeure in the state. Although there were exceptions that were quickly disappearing, the system remained feudal. When power was finally consolidated under Jiří of Poděbrady (and especially under Vladislaus after him), the Estates' representational government existed on one hand and the sovereign on the other. Even if the system remained feudal, power was divided between the three estates and the ruler, with the king no longer being an absolute sovereign in the same manner as during previous centuries. Towns were relegated to the background; their level of influence depended on military power derived from the decisive years of the Hussite Revolution (and later on, from its economic power). Affairs did not remain static, of course, and constant disputes over power arose between the Estates and the individual rulers, which effectively meant that the ruler was dependent on the Estates. This reality applied to everyone, including and especially beginning with Sigismund. And though Vladislaus attempted to subvert this arrangement and emancipate royal power, he actually failed to do so. The conflict intensified, especially with the arrival of the House of Habsburg on the Bohemian throne in 1526. The Habsburgs initially respected the Estates' power, but unfortunately the Counter-Reformation movement in the sixteenth century interfered with this organically developing relationship which seemed to have virtually no chance of manifesting any reactionary tendencies. In an empire which was experiencing pressure from political events, rulers had to respect the non-Catholic Estate's power, but they were unwilling to tolerate any kind of reform within the Kingdom of Bohemia. Even worse, the Habsburg monarchs increasingly underestimated the non-Catholic Bohemian Estates and the Electorate (not mentioning their encouraging conversions to Catholicism)—which would unfortunately lead to the tragic epilogue of the Estates monarchy, and culminated in the Second Defenestration of Prague in 1483 and the subsequent Bohemian Revolt (1618–1620). Based on previous legal traditions, Vaněček called the legal development of the second half of the fifteenth century (and that of the following century as well) a monarchical-estates dualism (*monarchia mixta*).[3]

The fact remained that various rulers continually wanted to preserve as much of the power and privileges which they normally possessed before the Hussite Revolution. On the other hand, the Estates were highly unwilling to surrender their rights and freedoms, given the long and arduous process required to gain them in the first place (whether through diplomacy or by the sword) and the fact that they wanted to exercise these powers themselves. In Bohemia, a distinctive feature of the strength of the Estates was their adherence to the laity receiving the chalice. This alone proves that their goals and aims were not purely the pursuit of materialistic advantages (i.e., the secularization of church property and holding onto royal property) but also spiritual "goods." Even for the most conservative Utraquist lords the chalice was not merely an appendage or an external sign of their reform efforts. Such a political approach would be more in line with contemporary times, but it certainly has no place in an age when religion still exercised a major role in the lives and history of states, nations, and individuals.

Vaněček is also of the opinion that the state apparatus at the time remained feudal in nature; thus, it made no difference if the power of the constituents was in the hands of the king or the Estates. That is a very relative position to hold, and even Vaněček had to admit that

> after the Hussite revolutionary movement, only quite exceptionally was a completely representative government reached—that is, where the sovereign would stand on one side against the Estates on the other side—as equals—and all three estates would be in balance with equal relations: the lords, the knights, and the towns. For the majority of that time, only the nobility ruled, and the dominance of the lords (of which the king was first and foremost a representative) normally prevailed.[4]

Although this is essentially true, at the same time one must note that during the course of the Hussite uprising the higher nobility suffered a significant blow to their governing power, from which they could never fully recover. Additionally, the king was not merely a representative of "nobility" but of all the estates combined. Consequently, any return to the previous state of affairs under Václav IV or his father (whose reign was often idealized) was virtually impossible.

Though the ascension of towns to power during the sixteenth century exceeds the limits of this study, some important facts need to be mentioned. First, it was not merely the general economic development which allowed towns to prosper and attain influence; most of the towns were also Utraquist, which means that they preserved the Hussite tradition and enjoyed quite a significant degree of popularity among the populace. Second, the relationship between the three estates was obviously and undeniably very complex. If one were to analyze the post-Hussite era, it could be asserted that the state apparatus formally remained feudal, but was also trying to break free from this condition at the same time. The so-called "Royal Council" can certainly be described as an organ responsible for the restoration of state administration from the time it first appeared with Sigismund in 1436. Its members consisted of lords and knights in a certain proportion without any town representatives in their ranks. While this Royal Council did play an important role in subsequent times, it was not an exclusive one since it was simply no longer possible to rule without inviting the burghers to participate. Although the nobility achieved several significant milestones in the common course of their struggle against the burghers at the time, they eventually lost their level of importance. The operation of the Provincial Court again in 1487, where the high and low nobility joined forces in their struggle for power against the king, towns, and commoners, enacted measures against serfs who had fled from their lord's domain.

The development of towns necessitated the promotion of freedom and the loosening of the feudal bonds:

The struggle against the estate of towns flared up immediately. The primary aim of the nobility was to expel representatives of royal towns from the Land Diet. At the same time, however, townspeople were prevented from acquiring property, they were bullied by extraneous lawsuits which brought them before royal courts, and finally, the nobles started to retract their recognition of certain production monopolies that the burghers possessed—such as brewing and selling beer.[5]

Another important factor for further legal developments was the prohibition of migration for serfs (both into different domains and into towns) without prior permission of their liege lord in 1487. In addition, the Diet stipulated in 1497 that those serfs who had deserted or fled after 1466 were obligated to return to the original domain to which they belonged. These measures undoubtedly sought to stall or even reverse the course of this progress; their attempts, however, only led to partial success, because the waves of development could not be suppressed so easily. The decision reached by Vladislaus's Provincial Code in 1500 implied a major victory for the nobility, because towns had to defend their rights to even a further extent. Nevertheless, the mutual compromise from 1517 called the *Svatováclavská smlouva* (The Saint Václav's Day Treaty) was a step forward as well as proof that those rights which were gained in the Hussite period could not be eradicated or eliminated. The nobility taught the towns how to make economic concessions, but in turn the towns made several demands of their own in the political sphere and taught the nobility how to make political concessions (e.g., towns being granted the right to be represented at Land Diets). Moreover, the 1540s witnessed a renewed rise of towns in terms of power and influence. This was indisputably part of the legacy of the Hussite epoch, as was the first uprising against the House of Habsburg which was predominantly led by towns in 1546–1547. This uprising was notable not only for being anti-feudal in nature but also for its confessional character. Needless to say, the Bohemian nobles went to great pains to distance themselves from the uprising once its looming defeat became obvious.

One of the institutions which forever transformed the Kingdom of Bohemia in the post-Hussite period (and which was in large part the result of the Hussites's efforts for an alternative new state) was the Bohemian Land Diet. Although the Diet itself was an estates-driven institution, its roots stretch back to the thirteenth century when the Crown lands were still ruled by the Přemysl dynasty. In its original pre-Hussite form this institution functioned predominantly as an advisory body rather than an executive body, although according to Vaněček the standing of the spiritual estate (or rather its highest representatives) was vague and uncertain.[6]

Thanks to the Hussite movement, the Bohemian Land Diets were given a more concrete form and more authority. In addition to transforming the feudal system, they would prove to be one of the most powerful political forces even on a European scale, eventually and incontrovertibly shaping the future. After the main phase of the Hussite movement ended with the election of Sigismund as King of Bohemia in 1436, the Diet was composed of three estates: the lords, the knights, and the royal towns.

> The lords and the knights had every right for personal participation and election . . . towns could only participate via delegates of their respective town councils . . . the Land Diet was convened by the King of Bohemia or (during times of *interregnum*) by his representatives, such as governors, vice-regents, etc. Each diet discussed either royal proposals or the initiatives brought forward by its participants. Sometimes each estate acted separately, each in their own curia, and at other times the Diet acted in plenary with the participation of all three estates. In principle, a valid resolution of the Diet was reached only when all three estates were in necessary agreement, although each individual curia of the Diet was usually determined by a majority of votes. An exception occurred around 1500 when weak rulers governed and the resolutions of the Diet were automatically presented to the king to be signed and then registered in the *Zemské desky* (*Landtafel*; literally translated as *Land tables*).[7]

As Malý describes in his research concerning Czech law, legal documents derived from the Bohemian Diet were gradually codified.[8] However, the development of central authorities and common state institutions of the Bohemian Crown over time remains an area which requires further research. As already noted, the neighboring Lands of the Bohemian Crown did not undergo the Hussite Reformation, so their situation differed drastically from the rest of the kingdom. Despite that fact, their central authorities and institutions still functioned and were also influenced to a significant extent by the Hussite struggle. One example is the office of royal prosecutor, which only appeared from the Hussite period onward and "whose origin was undoubtedly related to the efforts to consolidate and recover the claimed property which belonged to the king, to enforce the payment of a royal pension rightfully owed to the king, and to demand back any royal goods wrongfully acquired by the nobility."[9]

In summary, the historical evidence leads to the conclusion that the Hussite movement exercised a major influence in the struggle to determine a new form of state and its legal norms, even to the point where legal developments in the Lands of the Bohemian Crown (i.e., before, during, and after the Hussite period) were intricately connected with the movement's struggle for the freedom of individuals and society. This legal development is not only connected with Hussitism in all of its major periods but also with the entire Bohemian Reformation—all the way from its very beginning to the times of

Jan Hus and finally to its tragic end in 1620. The unifying program of this reformation was summarized in the *Four Articles of Prague*, which existed (with various modifications) until the victory of the Counter-Reformation. The legal historian Vaněček was well aware of how disastrous the acceptance the House of Habsburg on the throne was for the Estates-driven state, but unfortunately he did not take into account the religious perspective and the connection between the Bohemian Reformation (i.e., the Hussite legacy) and societal development. In his view, the election of the House of Habsburg signified the union of feudalism and Catholicism as political forces to serve the nobility. Although one can certainly admit the feudal restorative forces, the aggressive Counter-Reformation certainly was not yet present in the Lands of the Bohemian Crown in 1526, since its front only began gaining ground after the Council of Trent (1545–1563).

Similar to the later European Reformation, the Bohemian Reformation transformed not only the cultural but also the philosophical and legal horizon and constituted a major contribution toward the individualization of the law. The legal aspects (and not only from the perspective of constitutional law) of the Bohemian Reformation remain an engaging and rewarding topic of academic research. One of its greatest strengths is that it can provide a model for investigating and discovering legal rights within the complex postmodern age where states and nations are searching for a tolerable and beneficial form of contemporary coexistence.

NOTES

1. On the developments in state administration and government, see Malý et al., *Dějiny českého a československého.*
2. Vaněček, *Dějiny státu a práva v Československu do roku 1945,* 144.
3. Ibid.
4. Ibid., 145.
5. Ibid., 146–147.
6. Ibid., 154.
7. Ibid.
8. Malý et al., *Dějiny českého a československého,* 102–104.
9. Ibid., 67.

Bibliography

Bartoš, František Michálek. *Čechy v době Husově 1378–1415.* Prague: Jan Laichter, 1947.

———. *Do čtyř pražských artikuluů: Z myšlenkových a ústavních zápasuů let 1415–1420.* Prague: Nákladem Blahoslavovy společnosti, 1940.

———. *Husitská revoluce: Doba Žižkova 1415–1426,* vol. 1. Prague: Nakladatelství Československé akademie věd, 1965.

———. *Husitská revoluce: Vláda bratrstev a její pád 1426–1437,* vol. 2. Prague: Academia, 1966.

———. "Zikmund Korybutovič v Čechách." In *Sborník historický* 6 (1959): 171–221.

Baum, Wilhelm. *Kaiser Sigismund: Hus, Konstanz und Türkenkriege.* Graz-Wien-Köln: Styria, 1993.

Baum, Wilhelm and Kavka, František, eds. *Císař Zikmund: Kostnice, Hus a války proti Turkům.* Translated by Danuše Martinová and Pavel Kocek. Prague: Mladá fronta, 1996.

Betts, R.R. "Social and Constitutional Development in Bohemia in the Hussite Period." In *Past & Present,* 7/1 (1955): 37–54.

Boubín, Jaroslav, ed. *Jan z Příbrameě: Život kněžií Táborských.* Podbrdsko, Fontes 1. Příbram: Státní okresní archiv. Příbram: Okresní muzeum Příbram, 2000.

Buben, Milan. *Encyklopedie českých a moravských sídelních biskupů.* Prague: Logik, 2000.

Burdová, Pavla. *Desky zemské Království českého.* Prague: Státní ústřední archiv v Praze, 1990.

Čechura, Jaroslav. *České země v letech 1437–1526. I. díl, Mezi Zikmundem a Jiřím z Poděbrad (1437–1471).* Prague: Libri, 2010.

Cironis, Petros, ed. *Život a dílo Mistra Jana z Rokycan: svědectví Zdeňka Nejedlého, Kamila Krofty, Martina Kozáka a Josefa Teigeho.* Rokycany: Státní okresní archiv, 1997.

Čornej, Petr. *Velké dějiny zemí koruny české.* Sv. V. 1402–1437. Prague–Litomyšl: Paseka, 2000.

Čornej, Petr and Bártlová, Milena. *Světla a stíny husitství: (události, osobnosti, texty, tradice): výbor z úvah a studií.* Prague: NLN, Nakladatelství Lidové noviny, 2011.

———. *Velké dějiny zemí koruny české,* vol. 6 (1437–1526). Prague–Litomyšl: Paseka, 2007.

Čornejová, Ivana et al. *Dějiny Univerzity Karlovy.* vol. 1 *(1347/48–1622).* Prague: Univerzita Karlova, 1995.

Decaluwé, Michiel, Izbicki, Thomas M., and Christianson, Gerald, eds. *A Companion to the Council of Basel.* Leiden: Brill, 2016.

Farský, Karel. *Stát a církev: poměr státu českého k církvi římské od prvopočátku až do roku 1924.* V Praze: K. Farský, 1924.

Flajšhans, Václav, ed. *Spisy M. Jana Husi,* vol. 6, *Super IV Sententiarum.* Prague: Vilímek, 1906.

Goll, Jaroslav et al. *Fontes Rerum Bohemicarum,* vol. 3. Prague: Nákladem nadání Františka Palackého, 1882.

———. *Fontes Rerum Bohemicarum,* vol. 5. Prague: Nákladem Nadání Františka Palackého: V komissí knihkupectví Edv. Valečky, 1893.

Grygiel, Jerzy. *Zygmunt Korybutowicz: Litewski książę w husyckich Czechach (ok. 1395 wrzesien 1435).* Kraków: Avalon, 2016.

———. *Życie i działalność Zygmunta Korybutowicza. Studium z dziejów stosunków polsko-czeskich w pierwszej polowie XV wieku.* Wrocław-Warsaw-Krakow-Gdańsk-Lódź: Ossolineum, 1988.

Heymann, Frederick Gotthold. *George of Bohemia, King of Heretics.* Princeton: Princeton University Press, 1965.

Hrejsa, Ferdinand. *Dějiny křesťanství v Československu: Za krále Vladislava a Ludvíka. Před světovou reformací a za reformace,* vol. 6. Prague: Husova československá evangelická fakulta bohoslovecká, 1948.

Hus, Jan. *Spisy M. Jana Husi. Korespondence a dokumenty.* Prague: Komise pro vydávání pramenů náboženského hnutí čes., 1920.

———. *Husova výzbroj do Kostnice; Řeč o míru; O postačitelnosti Kristova zákona; Řeč o víře; Prohlášení o článcích Pálčových.* Translated by Amedeo Molnár and František Mrázek Dobiáš. (1st edition). Prague: Ústřední církevní nakladatelství, 1965.

Kadlec, Jaroslav. *Mistr Vojtěch Raňkův z Ježova.* Prague: Univerzita Karlova, 1969.

Kaminsky, Howard. *A History of the Hussite Revolution.* Berkeley: University of California Press, 1967.

Kavka, František. *Poslední Lucemburk na českém trůně: králem uprostřed revoluce.* Prague: Mladá fronta, 1998.

Kejř, Jiří. *Husitský právník M. Jan z Jesenice.* Prague: Nakladatelství Československé akademie věd, 1965.

———. *Husité.* Prague: Panorama, 1984.

———. *Husovo odvolání od soudu papežova k soudu Kristovu.* Ústí nad Labem: Albis international, 1999.

———. *Husův proces.* Prague: Vyšehrad, 2000.

———. "Jan Hus jako právní myslitel." In Lášek, Jan Blahoslav, ed. et al. *Jan Hus mezi epochami, národy a konfesemi: sborník z mezinárodního sympozia, konaného*

22–26. září 1993 v Bayreuthu, SRN, 197–207. Prague: Česká křesťanská akademie, 1995.

———. "Johannes Hus als Rechtsdenker." In *Jan Hus—Zwischen Zeiten, Völkern, Konfessionen: Vorträge des internationalen Symposions in Bayreuth vom 22. bis 26. September 1993*, Ferdinand Seibt et al., eds., 213–226. München: R. Oldenbourg, 1997.

Krchňák, Alois. *Čechové na Basilejském sněmu*. Řím: Křesťanská akad., 1967.

———. *Čechové na basilejském sněmu* (2nd edition). Trinitas první. Svitavy: Trinitas, 1997.

Kurz, Friedrich, *Österreich unter K. Albrecht dem Zweyten*, Wien: Kupffer und Singer, 1835.

Kybal, Vlastimil. *M. Jan Hus: život a učení. Díl 2, Učení*. Prague: Jan Laichter, 1923–1931.

Lášek, Jan Blahoslav. "Kněz Ambrož a východočeské husitství, Hradec a Oreb." In *Theologická revue UK HTF* 70 (1999): 45–57.

———. "Priest Ambrož and East-Bohemian Utraquism: Hradec and Oreb." In *The Bohemian Reformation and Religious Practice*, vol. 3, eds. Zdeněk V. David and David R. Holeton, 105–118. Prague: Academy of Sciences of the Czech Republic, 2000.

Lupáč, Martin and Císařová-Kolářová, Anna, eds. *Hádání o kompaktátech*. Prague: Ústřední církevní nakladatelství, 1953.

Macek, Josef, ed. *Ktož jsú boží bojovníci: čtení o Taboře v husitském revolučním hnutí*. Prague: Melantrich, 1951.

———. *Tábor v husitském revolučním hnutí. I. díl* (2nd edition). Prague: ČSAV, 1956.

———. *Tábor v husitském revolučním hnutí. II. díl, Tábor chudiny venkovské a městské*. Prague: Nakladatelství Československé akademie věd, 1955.

František Ryšánek et al., eds. *Magistri Iohannis Hus Opera Omnia*. 25 vols. Prague: Academia, 1959–.

Malý, Jakub, *Vlastenecký slovník historický*, Prague: Rohlíček a Sievers, 1877.

Malý, Karel. "Die Bibel und das hussitische Rechtsdenken." In *Jan Hus—Zwischen Zeiten, Völkern, Konfessionen: Vorträge des internationalen Symposions in Bayreuth vom 22. bis 26. September 1993*, Ferdinand Seibt et al., eds., 227–234. München: R. Oldenbourg, 1997.

———. "K právnímu odkazu husitství." In Lášek, Jan Blahoslav, ed. et al. *Jan Hus mezi epochami, národy a konfesemi: sborník z mezinárodního sympozia, konaného 22.–26. září 1993 v Bayreuthu, SRN*, 208–212. Prague: Česká křesťanská akademie, 1995.

———. *Trestní právo v Čechách v 15–16. století*. Prague: Univerzita Karlova, 1979.

——— et al. *Dějiny českého a československého práva do roku 1945*. Prague: Leges, 2010.

Molnár, Amedeo. "Chebský soudce." In *Soudce smluvený v Chebu: sborník příspěvků přednesených na symposiu k 550. výročí*, 2–75. Prague: Panorama, 1982.

———. *Valdenští: evropský rozměr jejich vzdoru* (2nd edition). Prague: Kalich, 1991.

Novotný, Václav. *Hus v Kostnici a česká šlechta: poznámky a dokumenty*. Prague: Nákladem Společnosti přátel starožitností českých v Praze, 1915.

———. *M. Jana Husi Korespondence a dokumenty*. Prague: Nákladem komise pro vydávání pramenů náboženského hnutí českého, 1920.

Odložilík, Otakar. *The Hussite King: Bohemia in European Affairs 1440–1471*. New Brunswick: Rutgers University Press, 1965.

Palacký, František, ed. *Archiv český, čili, Staré písemné památky české i morawske [sic]: z archivůw domácích i cizích*, vol. 3. W Praze: [Stawy Králowstwj Českého], 1844.

———. *Archiv český, čili, Staré písemné památky české i morawske: z archivůw domácích i cizích*, vol. 3. Prague: Stawy Králowstwj Českého, 1844.

———. *Urkundliche Beiträge zur Geschichte des Hussitenkrieges in den Jahren 1419–1436*, Band II., Prague: Friedrich Tempsky, 1873.

Petr Žatecký, *Deník Petra Žateckého (Liber diurnus)*. Translated by František Heřmanský. Prague: Melantrich, 1953.

Říčan, Rudolf et al., eds. *Čtyři vyznání: vyznání Augsburské, Bratrské, Helvetské a České: Se 4 vyznáními staré církve a se Čtyřmi články praž*. Prague: Komenského evangelická fakulta bohoslovecká, 1951.

Ryantová, Marie, Vorel, Petr, and Antonín, Robert, eds. *Čeští králové*. Prague: Paseka, 2008.

Ryba, Bohumil, ed. *Magistri Iohannis Hus Quodlibet*. Prague: Orbis, 1948.

Salač, Antonín. *Constantinople et Prague en 1452: [pourparlers en vue d'une union des Eglises] = Cařihrad a Praha r. 1452: [jednání o církevní unii]*. Prague: ČSAV, 1958.

Schatz, Klaus. *Všeobecné koncily: ohniska církevních dějin*. Brno: Centrum pro studium demokracie a kultury (CDK), 2014.

Šimek, František. *Učení M. Jana Rokycany*. Prague: Nákladem České akademie věd a umění, 1938.

———. Jan Rokycana, *Postilla*, 2 vols. Prague: České Akademii Věd a Umění, 1928–1929.

Šmahel, František. *Basilejská kompaktáta: příběh deseti listin*. Vyd. 1. Prague: NLN, Nakladatelství Lidové noviny, 2011.

Šmahel, František et al. *Dějiny Tábora*, 2 vols. České Budějovice: Jihočeské nakladatelství, 1988–1990.

———. *Husitská revoluce. I, Doba vymknutá z kloubů*. Prague: Historický ústav AV ČR, 1993.

———. *Husitská revoluce. II, Kořeny české reformace*. Prague: Historický ústav AV ČR, 1993.

———. *Husitská revoluce. III, Kronika válečných let*. Prague: Historický ústav AV ČR, 1993.

———. *Husitská revoluce. IV, Epilog bouřlivého věku*. Prague: Historický ústav AV ČR, 1993.

Spinka, Matthew. *John Hus at the Council of Constance*. New York: Columbia University Press, 1965.

Svoboda, Milan, ed. *Mistra Jakoubka ze Stříbra Překlad Viklefova dialogu*. Prague: Česká akademie císaře Františka Josefa pro vědy, slovesnost a umění, 1909.

Tanner, Norman P., ed. *Decrees of the Ecumenical Councils*. Washington, DC: Georgetown University Press, 1990.

Tomek, Václav Vladivoj. *Děje university pražské*. Prague: W kommissí u Řiwnáče, 1849.

Urbánek, Rudolf. *České dějiny. Díl III, Věk poděbradský*, 4 vols. Prague: Jan Laichter, 1915–1962.

Vaněček, Václav. *Dějiny státu a práva v Československu do roku 1945: vysokoškolská učebnice* (3rd edition). Prague: Orbis, 1976.

de Vooght, Paul. *L'hérésie de Jean Huss*, 2 vols. Louvain: Bureaux de la revue bibliothèque de l'université, 1975.

———. *Jacobellus de Stribro (†1429). premier théologien du hussitisme*. Louvain: Publications universitaires de Louvain, 1972.

Vošahlíková, Pavla et al. *Bibliografický slovník českých zemí*. Prague: Libri, 2004.

Index

About the Author and Translator

Kamila Veverková works as the dean of the Hussite Theological Faculty of Charles University in Prague. She has written significant monographs on Anton Krombholz and Bernard Bolzano and his circle.

Angelo Shaun Franklin is an independent researcher who works as a translator and educational consultant in Prague. He is currently translating several theological texts by Jan Hus and other medieval Bohemian works.